D1163996

FROM RAJ TO RAJIV

40 YEARS OF
INDIAN INDEPENDENCE

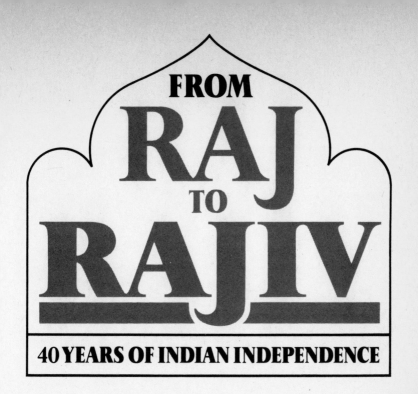

FROM RAJ TO RAJIV

40 YEARS OF INDIAN INDEPENDENCE

MARK TULLY
·
ZAREER MASANI

BBC BOOKS

The cartoon on page 45 is
by R. K. Laxman in *The Times of India*
and is reproduced by kind permission.

Published by BBC Books
A division of BBC Enterprises Ltd
Woodlands, 80 Wood Lane
London W12 0TT

First published 1988

© Mark Tully and Zareer Masani 1988

ISBN 0 563 20629 2

Photoset in 11/12pt Sabon and printed in Great Britain by
Redwood Burn Limited, Trowbridge, Wiltshire

CONTENTS

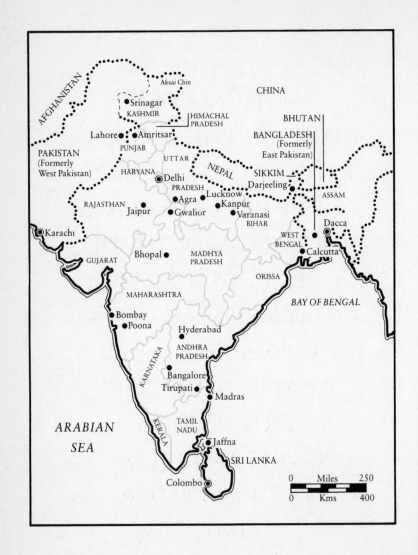

PREFACE

The title *From Raj to Rajiv* implies a comprehensive history of independent India. It is not. The radio programmes, and this book which is based on them, could perhaps best be described as appetisers. They are an attempt to arouse interest in India and to increase sympathetic understanding of its aspirations and its problems. Inevitably that has meant describing those problems, but the book is by no means just a catalogue of woes. Many listeners have told me that they found the radio programmes optimistic, and I hope that this optimism will get through to readers too. Indian civilisation is much older than our own, and I am sure that the Indian people will see that it survives for many centuries more. My favourite character in the book is the dock worker who has spent his life living under a plastic sheet on the pavements of Bombay yet still retains his optimism and his ambitions for his family. I go along with the constitutional lawyer who puts his trust in the 'common man' and says it is the 'common man' who will in the end discipline the politician.

We from the prosperous and democratic West take little interest in India's problems because they barely touch our lives. When the London stock market collapses, no one asks what is happening on Dalal Street, Bombay's stock exchange. When nuclear disarmament is discussed, the potential nuclear arms race in South Asia barely gets a hearing. Even India's low-cost labour doesn't pose a great threat to our jobs. We have our rich men's clubs and our rich men's defence pacts, and India is very much not a member of them. Yet we believe in democracy, and so India's struggle to preserve democracy, against odds which no Western nation faces, should surely interest us.

All too often, listeners and readers in the West get the impression that the poorer countries of the world are either incompetent or unwilling to help themselves. They are portrayed as depending on our aid and our charity. I wonder how many people in Britain realise that in 1986 we signed orders worth £300 million for the supply of defence equipment to India and committed ourselves to give just £100 million in aid. In the same year, the balance of trade between the two countries was £500 million in our favour. So India is in no way a net receiver of our aid or charity. What is more, India has never run up debts which it was unable to pay. In fact, British and American banks are falling over each other in their anxiety to lend to India because its credit worthiness is so high. India is entirely self-reliant, determined to solve its own problems and not to be dependent on anyone else's charity. India does not disguise what one senior civil servant in this book calls the 'stupendous challenges' the nation faces – it must surely be one of the most open and self-critical societies in the world – but criticism has not led to despair. That is the message I got from the interviews we recorded to make *From Raj to Rajiv*.

Radio programmes with presenters leave listeners with the impression that they are one person's work. In this case nothing could be further from the truth. The programmes were a partnership between myself and my producer, Zareer Masani, and we shared the writing of this book. Many of the interviews were recorded by Anne Howells of the BBC, for whose help I am grateful. My long-suffering colleagues in the BBC's Delhi Office and Gillian Wright have put in many extra hours on *From Raj to Rajiv*. The real stars of the radio programmes are the many Indians, some internationally distinguished in their fields, who willingly gave up their time to record interviews. To them we owe the programmes and this book. In a country like India, where there is such wealth of human talent, we had to make very difficult choices. I hope we have chosen well.

Mark Tully
New Delhi
January 1988

CHRONOLOGY

1947

15 AUGUST Indian independence day.
OCTOBER Kashmir crisis. First war with Pakistan.

1948

30 JANUARY Assassination of Mahatma Gandhi.
MARCH Communists begin campaign to attempt to overthrow the state by violence. Campaign lasts for 3½ years.
JUNE Mountbatten leaves India. Appointment of first Indian Governor-General.
SEPTEMBER Indian forces sent into Hyderabad state. The Nizam accedes to the Union.

1949

APRIL India decides to remain in the Commonwealth as a Republic.

1950

26 JANUARY Republic of India inaugurated.
Planning Commission created.
DECEMBER Sardar Vallabhai Patel dies.

1951

JULY India's first Five-Year Plan published.
SEPTEMBER India's President, Rajendra Prasad, threatens to resign over Hindu Code Bill.
OCTOBER–MARCH 1952 First general elections.

1953

AUGUST Sheikh Abdullah's government in Kashmir dismissed and Abdullah arrested.

OCTOBER Formation of Andhra Pradesh, India's first linguistic state.

1954

APRIL Sino-Indian agreement on Tibet whereby India recognises Tibet as part of China.

JUNE Chou En-lai visits Delhi. Joint statement on principles of peace.

1955

JANUARY Congress declares that 'socialistic pattern of society' is the objective of planning.

FEBRUARY Economic assistance from the USSR inaugurated with the announcement of the building of a steel mill.

Indira Gandhi becomes a member of Congress Working Committee.

APRIL Bandung Conference.

OCTOBER States Reorganisation Commission submits its report. Recommends the formation of further linguistic states.

1956

OCTOBER Nehru condemns Suez but not the suppression of the Hungarian Uprising.

NOVEMBER States Reorganisation Bill passed.

1957

FEBRUARY-MARCH Second general elections. India's first Communist government elected in Kerala.

1958

OCTOBER India protests to China over Aksai Chin road.

1959

JANUARY Mrs Gandhi elected President of the Congress Party.

Chou En-lai lays claim to large areas of Indian territory.

MARCH Dalai Lama flees Tibet.

JULY Kerala government dismissed.

1960

JULY Forward Policy adopted in border areas.
SEPTEMBER Feroze Gandhi, Indira's husband, dies.
DECEMBER Indian forces invade Goa.

1962

JANUARY Third general elections.
20 OCTOBER Chinese offensive launched on eastern and western fronts.
7 NOVEMBER Nehru accepts Defence Minister Krishna Menon's resignation from the Cabinet.
21 NOVEMBER China announces unilateral ceasefire.

1963

AUGUST Many of Nehru's senior Cabinet colleagues, including Morarji Desai, resign under the Kamaraj Plan to work for the party.

1964

JANUARY Nehru suffers stroke.
27 MAY Nehru dies. Shastri becomes Prime Minister and Mrs Gandhi Minister of Information and Broadcasting.
AUGUST Indira Gandhi elected to Parliament (Rajya Sabha or Upper House) for the first time.
OCTOBER–NOVEMBER Communist Party of India splits.

1965

1 SEPTEMBER Second Indo–Pakistan War starts. Lasts 22 days.

1966

10 JANUARY Shastri dies after signing the Tashkent Agreement.
24 JANUARY Indira Gandhi sworn in as Prime Minister.
6 JUNE Indian rupee devalued by 35.5% under World Bank pressure.

1967

FEBRUARY Fourth general elections. Mrs Gandhi forced to accept Morarji Desai as Deputy Prime Minister.
MAY Mrs Ghandi announces 10-point programme including bank nationalisation and abolition of maharajas' privy purses and privileges.

1969

JULY–NOVEMBER Crisis in Congress Party leading to split.

1970

SEPTEMBER Legislation abolishing privy purses defeated in Rajya Sabha, the Upper House of Parliament. Mrs Gandhi issues ordinance.

DECEMBER Mrs Gandhi dissolves Parliament and calls mid-term parliamentary elections.

1971

MARCH Mrs Gandhi wins two-thirds majority in the Lok Sabha, the Lower House of Parliament.

25 MARCH Pakistan army begins military crackdown in East Pakistan. Refugees start fleeing across the border.

AUGUST Mrs Gandhi signs Treaty of Peace, Friendship and Co-operation with the USSR.

3 DECEMBER Pakistan Air Force launches attack on Indian air bases. Third Indo–Pakistan War breaks out.

16 DECEMBER Pakistan army commander surrenders in Dhaka.

1972

JUNE Simla Summit. Mrs Gandhi and Prime Minister Z. A. Bhutto of Pakistan sign Simla Agreement.

1973

APRIL Mrs Gandhi breaks the tradition of appointing the Chief Justice on the basis of seniority.

1974

MARCH JP Movement in Bihar starts.

MAY Railway strike.

'Peaceful' nuclear explosion.

1975

JUNE Mrs Gandhi found guilty of corrupt electoral practices by Allahabad High Court.

25/26 JUNE Emergency imposed.

15 AUGUST Sheikh Mujibur Rahman, President of Bangladesh, assassinated.

1976

NOVEMBER Term of Lok Sabha extended so that parliamentary elections not necessary until March 1978.

1977

JANUARY Mrs Gandhi's surprise announcement that elections will be held.

MARCH Mrs Gandhi defeated in election and lifts Emergency before resigning. Janata Party government formed under Morarji Desai, India's first non-Congress Prime Minister.

1978

JUNE Continuing row over leadership of Janata Party leads to Home Minister, Charan Singh, leaving the government.

JULY Morarji Desai forced to take Charan Singh back as Finance Minister.

NOVEMBER Mrs Gandhi returns to Parliament by winning by-election in southern state of Karnataka.

1979

JULY Janata government falls. Charan Singh succeeds as caretaker Prime Minister.

DECEMBER Soviet forces enter Afghanistan.

1980

JANUARY Mrs Gandhi wins general elections.

JUNE Sanjay Gandhi killed in air crash.
Rajiv Gandhi enters politics.

1981

SEPTEMBER Sant Jarnail Singh Bhindranwale arrested and then released. The Sikh religious party, the Akali Dal, and Bhindranwale join hands.

1982

SEPTEMBER Sheikh Abdullah dies.

NOVEMBER Asian Games in Delhi. Checks on Sikhs entering capital cause widespread resentment.

1983

FEBRUARY Nellie massacre during Assam state elections.

APRIL Assassination of Deputy Inspector-General of Police Atwal at Golden Temple in Amritsar.

1984

JUNE Operation Blue Star.

31 OCTOBER Assassination of Mrs Gandhi. Delhi riots. Rajiv succeeds as Prime Minister.

3 DECEMBER Bhopal gas disaster.

DECEMBER–JANUARY 1985 Rajiv Gandhi wins largest ever majority for Congress in general elections.

1985

24 JULY Punjab Accord.

SEPTEMBER Punjab state elections. Akali Dal government formed.

31 DECEMBER Rajiv Gandhi makes speech critical of Congress at Congress Centenary celebrations in Bombay.

1986

30 APRIL Chief Minister of Punjab orders security forces to enter the Golden Temple complex. This causes split in Akali Dal, threatening Punjab Accord.

2 OCTOBER Assassination attempt on Rajiv Gandhi.

NOVEMBER Gorbachev visits India.

1987

12 APRIL Defence Minister, V. P. Singh, resigns over row about government corruption.

11 MAY Rajiv Gandhi dismisses Punjab government, signifying the collapse of the Punjab Accord.

JUNE Congress Party routed in elections to the Haryana state assembly.

JULY Accord with Sri Lanka. Indian army peacekeeping force sent to Jaffna.

IMPERIAL INHERITANCE

At midnight, on 14 August 1947, the curtain came down on the British Raj in India. The moment was marked by a stirring ceremony in the Central Hall of what was then India's Constituent Assembly. An imposing, circular, sandstone building built for the exclusive Legislative Assembly of the Raj in the Indo-Baroque style of Sir Edwin Lutyens, it now houses the parliament of independent India. The chimes of midnight were greeted by a fanfare of conch-shells, and then a female choir sang the Sanskrit nationalist anthem, '*Vande Mataram*' ('I bow to thee, my motherland'). The high point of the ceremony was a lyrical speech by independent India's first prime minister, Jawaharlal Nehru. 'Long years ago,' he began, 'we made a tryst with destiny. And now the time comes when we shall redeem our pledge, not wholly or in full measure, but very substantially. At the stroke of the midnight hour, when the world sleeps, India will awake to life and freedom.'

Nehru's independence speech has gone down in history as a masterpiece of political rhetoric. But the great Urdu poet, Faiz Ahmed Faiz, was less enthusiastic. He described independence as 'a scarred daybreak, a night-bitten dawn'; and at first he appeared to be right.

The price of independence had been the partition of the sub-continent into two new states with religious boundaries that made geographical nonsense. The Muslim-majority areas of British India were to form the Islamic state of Pakistan; the rest would continue to be India. Partition was intended to avert the threat of civil war between Hindus and Muslims. But its architects failed to anticipate the sectarian massacres and forced migration to which they were condemning Hindu and Muslim minorities left behind in the divided territories.

On the very day that Nehru dedicated himself to the service of the Indian people, and to the still larger cause of humanity, riots broke out in Punjab on both sides of the new border – at Amritsar in India and Lahore in Pakistan. Nobody knows how many people were killed in the terrible holocaust that followed partition. Some estimate 200 000, some 400 000, and some a million.

For the *Sahibs* and *Mem-Sahibs* who had constituted the Raj, independence proved far less traumatic. Twenty years earlier, few would have anticipated or admitted that their days in India were numbered; but when the moment came, they packed up and left with surprisingly little rancour or heartache. Many in the services firmly declined invitations from India's new rulers to stay on and share their experience and wisdom with the new administration.

India, after all, had never been home to the British rulers, the vast majority of whom had always intended to return to Britain. They had come to India to rule or administer justice, to do business or build bridges, and had then retired to Bognor Regis or Budleigh Salterton, to Cheltenham or Chalfont St Giles. Staying on had been very rare and strongly disapproved of; going 'jungli', or native, had been an unforgivable crime in the social code of empire.

Because the Raj always went home to retire, there were no influential white settlers in India to oppose Independence, as there were in Rhodesia and Kenya. That perhaps is one reason why the British did not even have to be pushed in the end. There are prominent Indian historians and political commentators who argue that the British cut and ran when it suited them, that the hurried post-war transfer of power had less to do with democratic principles than with Britain's reluctance to commit the military and financial resources that a more orderly and long-drawn withdrawal would have required.

Both Nehru and Mohammed Ali Jinnah, the founder of Pakistan, preferred partition to the alternative of a loose federation which had been proposed by the Cabinet Mission, sent out by the British Government in 1945. Minoo Masani, who was a member of the Constituent Assembly at the time, attributes this to their impatience to assume undivided power, albeit in a divided sub-continent.

> I held the view that independence should have been postponed for the sake of getting it along with the unity of India. That was a minority point of view, but I was in very good company, because among those who held that view were Mahatma Gandhi and my good friend Jayaprakash Narayan.[1] But the majority of people, including Nehru and Patel,[2] were impatient and wanted the Muslims to get out, so they could be masters in their own homes without any further delay. The egotism of Jinnah on one side, and Nehru on the other, came in the way of a united India being independent. For instance, Gandhi's offer of the prime ministership to Jinnah, which would have solved the problem, was blocked by Nehru and Patel.

While he condemns the impatience of Indian leaders, Masani also blames the new Labour government in Britain, led by Clement Attlee, for shirking British responsibilities and leaving India in a mess.

> Mountbatten was sent by Attlee to do this job, and he did it with great panache. I would say that Mountbatten by scuttling, by withdrawing British troops, did a good job for Britain, but he did a lousy one for India.... Imperial powers which have ruled for over a century have no business to scuttle and leave things in a mess. The Belgians did it in the Congo, the Portuguese in Angola and Mozambique, and the British did it in India. You can't just walk out when it doesn't suit you any more; you have an obligation to people to leave them in good shape. And you can't withdraw your armed forces and let anarchy break loose, which is what happened.... I think if the British army had not been withdrawn, there'd have been no massacres of

1 Jayaprakash Narayan was the founder of the Indian Socialist Party and had led the 'Quit India' revolt against British rule in 1942–43.
2 Sardar Vallabhai Patel, who became Deputy Prime Minister of India, was one of the ruling triumvirate of Congress, along with Gandhi and Nehru.

the scale that actually took place, and this is confirmed by friends in the army who saw all this happening. They also felt that the withdrawal of the British armed forces was the key thing. With the British troops there, nothing much would have happened.

The conventional wisdom at the time, reiterated recently by Lord Mountbatten's biographer, Philip Ziegler, is that the last viceroy had no alternative, that a British refusal to partition and quit would have plunged the sub-continent into civil war.

> Obviously, there was an element of not being able to afford it any more, not being able to find the troops to police India any more. But I think it was far more a question of principle as far as the Labour government was concerned. I believe Attlee was totally convinced that India not merely could but should have immediate independence and was quite determined to implement it.... From the point of view of a Labour government, they just did not feel they could ask British forces to stay on, nor indeed would British forces have been ready to stay on.

Ziegler also rejects the view that Mountbatten would have done better to play for time and delay partition until the situation stabilised. 'I just do not see,' he declares emphatically, 'given the cards in his hand and the weakening of the situation every day, the growth of communal violence and the crumbling of the police and the judiciary and the army, that he could have done anything except push it through as fast as he possibly could.'

Whether an undivided India could have been brought to independence, and how long it would have lasted, must remain a matter for historical conjecture. What is certain, as Minoo Masani points out, is that an open civil war could scarcely have wrought more carnage and destruction than the upheavals triggered by partition.

> The price we paid is out of all proportion. There were about a million people killed on each side, thousands and thousands of women raped, an arms race that is

still going on today, which has impoverished both countries, two wars which have already taken place, and goodness knows how many more in the offing. Independence was not worth having at this price, and it was vitiated from the beginning by the way it was achieved.

In the period from 1947 to 1948, the flames of communal violence spread so far and so fast that the Indian Army, without the aid of British troops, was quite unable to contain it. One of the officers entrusted with this task was K. P. Candeth, who later retired as a general in independent India. He explains how difficult it was to prevent trainloads of refugees from being butchered like cattle.

> The major problem was to guard these trains, because when they stopped at night the local villagers used to attack them. The worst places were in Punjab. For instance, I remember seeing a train come in from Pakistan and there wasn't a single live person on it; there were just bodies, dead and butchered. Now, that train entered India, and the people saw it. And the next Pakistan-bound train that came, they set upon, and the slaughter was incredible.
>
> And then there were huge walking convoys ... people coming in across the border, millions, wounded, without food, without clothes, carrying what they could, just streaming across the border helter-skelter. And then inside, where you had Muslim pockets, you had to provide protection for them, because otherwise they would be slaughtered. And every time there was a slaughter on the other side, or trains and vehicles came with dead bodies, there was a reaction on this side. When there was a reaction on this side, there was another one on that side; and so it built up.

If Nehru, by his reluctance to share power with Jinnah, contributed to partition, he must have been all the more mortified by the violence that followed. He had always abhorred sectarian conflict and was entirely non-sectarian in his own outlook.

17

According to his private secretary, N. K. Seshan, his sympathy for Indian Muslims often irritated some of his Hindu colleagues, who used to refer to him as Maulana[1] Nehru. 'He felt Hindus were safe anyhow in India,' Seshan explains, 'but he felt minorities should be protected, even if the majority had to sacrifice something.'

It has been suggested that Nehru virtually collapsed in the face of the partition riots and handed responsibility back to Mountbatten, who by then had become the first Governor-General of independent India. But this is not how Seshan remembers Nehru at the time.

> Wherever there was a riot taking place, his immediate reaction was to go there personally, wherever it was. He was stopped only with difficulty from going into those places. And he would really get upset with the army commanders and others when they'd come back and report to him that they were unable to control the situation.... He would reprimand them, and he used to lose his temper very badly.

Nehru was quick to anger, but he was equally quick to forgive. He had his vanity, and revelled in the adulation of the crowds, liking nothing more than putting one over on security advisers who tried to keep the people at a distance. On one occasion, he confused his security men by driving behind the crowd. He later explained to his long-suffering Director of Intelligence that any potential assassin would have been standing in the front, where the police barricades were; so he had deceived the assassins and met the people. 'What do you think?' he asked gleefully. 'I think I'm cleverer than your policemen.'

Although the British boasted that it was they who had united India, they left behind a badly divided country, with both Hindus and Muslims overcome by a murderous madness. The only person who had any influence over the hate-filled Hindus of northern and eastern India was Mahatma Gandhi. His assassination by a Hindu fanatic, shortly after independence, so shamed the nation that the Hindus returned to their senses and the blood-letting ended. The man whom Churchill scornfully described as a half-naked *fakir*,[2] because he only

1 Maulana is a Muslim title for a scholar of Islamic theology.
2 The Muslim equivalent of a mendicant friar.

wore a loincloth to identify himself with the poor, was assassinated in the garden of Birla House, the Delhi home of India's richest business magnate. That, too, could be seen as having a symbolic significance, since Gandhi's life-mission had been to bring together all Indians, Hindus and Muslims, rich and poor.

The Mahatma's assassination marked the climax of the nightmare that partition had become. Major Singha, the officer in command of Mountbatten's Gurkha guards, describes the surreal way in which the news of Gandhi's death reached the country's head of state. Singha was walking along a road near the Governor-General's palace, when a passing student told him that *Bapu*,[1] as Gandhi was popularly known, had been killed. It took the major, who had spent his life in the political isolation of the British Indian army, a little while to work out whose *Bapu* this was. The Governor-General himself was out for his regular evening ride with his daughter, Lady Pamela Mountbatten, and his Prime Minister, Jawaharlal Nehru. Singha gave him the news when he got back. Fearing a major outbreak of violence if Gandhi's assassin turned out to be a Muslim, Mountbatten at once ordered his personal guard of 250 Gurkhas to take up positions around Birla House, where the Mahatma's body lay. Major Singha found the Gurkhas rather puzzled by all this fuss over the death of someone they had never heard of.

> While they were lining up, I gave a brief résumé of the situation to the Sergeant-Major and said 'Mahatma Gandhi has been assassinated.' He said: 'Never heard of him.' So I had to explain. I said: 'He was a great, world-famous leader and some bad man has gone and assassinated him.' And when as usual I asked if he had any questions, he said: 'Look, he must have run away with a woman or done something wrong. No one is going to assassinate him for nothing.'

For the Gurkhas, recruited and prized by the Raj because of their supreme contempt for Indian political aspirations, Gandhi's assassination might have been an insignificant event. But for India's Prime Minister, it meant the loss at one stroke

[1] 'Father'.

of a political mentor, a father-figure, and a much-loved friend and confidant. Nehru's secretary, Seshan, remembers telephoning him with the news: 'I told him that this is the message – he has been shot dead. For a minute, I didn't hear anything from him. Then he said "*Achhaa*" (all right) and put the telephone down. He came straight away to Birla House.'

Seshan says that Nehru broke down and wept at Birla House. But he soon pulled himself together, returned to his office and started dictating the broadcast to the nation he would be making later that evening. It was to be another of his great speeches, breaking the potentially explosive news of Gandhi's assassination in a deeply moving, yet controlled and consoling elegy, of which the Mahatma himself would surely have approved. 'The light has gone out of our lives,' Nehru announced in a voice laden with grief, 'and there is darkness everywhere. I do not quite know what to tell you and how to say it. Our beloved leader, *Bapu* as we called him, the father of the nation, is no more. Perhaps I am wrong to say that. Nevertheless, we will not see him again as we have seen him for these many years. We will not run to him for advice and seek solace from him. And that is a terrible blow, not to me only, but to millions and millions in this country.'

More than any other event, Gandhi's death purged the country of communal hatred, giving Nehru time to turn his attention to the task of building a new India. Alongside the vast refugee problem created by partition, there was the equally daunting diplomatic task of integrating more than five hundred nominally independent princely states into the Indian Union. Under the Raj, the princes had enjoyed a separate status from the provinces of British India, acknowledging the paramountcy of the British Crown, but otherwise autonomous in the administration of their own territories. These ranged in size from tiny enclaves of a few hundred square miles to large kingdoms like Kashmir in the north and Hyderabad in the south, bigger in area and population than many European nations. The situation was complicated by the fact that the religious partition of the sub-continent had left some princes in an anomalous position, notably the Hindu Maharaja of Muslim-majority Kashmir and the Muslim Nizam of Hindu-majority Hyderabad. Nevertheless, by 1950, when India became a republic, a combination of persuasion and arm-twisting had achieved what had seemed an impossible task. The architect of princely integration was not Nehru but his deputy, Sardar Vallabhai Patel, India's equivalent of an Iron Chancellor.

One of the leading princely states was the central Indian kingdom of Gwalior, whose loyalty to the British was probably decisive in defeating the Mutiny or Great Revolt of 1857. The Rajmata (Queen Mother) of Gwalior is today a prominent leader of the right-wing Hindu Bhartiya Janata Party, or B.J.P. Reflecting on those early days of independence, she complains that she and her husband were pushed with unnecessary haste into signing a merger agreement with India.

> There was quite a lot of pressure because they didn't want to give us too much time, so that we should not make it difficult for them. So they were trying to rush us through.... I remember the night we signed. Till 2 o'clock, Mr Menon[1] was sitting with me, trying to coax me to say 'yes'. Because my husband said: 'I wouldn't like to decide such an important issue alone. I would like my wife also to join me in this decision, and she is very reluctant.' So Mr Menon was sent to me.

The Rajmata says that her reluctance sprang not from any antipathy to Indian independence, which she welcomed, but from her anxiety that the interests of Gwalior state would be submerged in those of such a large Union. Nevertheless, Menon overcame her hesitation in those late-night talks, as he did with hundreds of other lesser princes.

In 1950, Sardar Patel died with his mission accomplished and India's unification completed. Although his death deprived the government of its most able administrator, it strengthened Nehru's hand politically. Patel had been his only serious rival in the Congress Party. Very much a Hindu traditionalist, he had been largely untouched by the Western influence which Nehru had imbibed at Harrow and Trinity College, Cambridge. Patel's earthy Indianness was much closer to Mahatma Gandhi's outlook than Nehru's anglicised political values. Yet, according to Professor Ravindra Kumar

[1] V. P. Menon, Patel's right-hand man, was the senior civil servant responsible for negotiating with the princes.

of the Nehru Museum in Delhi, Gandhi was being far-sighted when he chose Nehru, not Patel, as his political heir.

Patel was in so many ways ideologically and organisationally much closer to Gandhi than Jawaharlal Nehru. But Gandhi very wisely felt that these were not the only criteria necessary for a person who would succeed him.... No leader of India as a whole can represent only one class; it is not as if one is able to establish rapport with the peasantry, and that suffices. Nehru had links with other sections of our society. For instance, the younger generations of the twenties and thirties, he had a special link with them and with the intelligentsia. It is also important to remember that, if a particular leader is too closely tied to one region, he cannot be an All India leader. Jawaharlal came from a social background which was very élite, that didn't have roots in any one of the Indian regions, but belonged to the country as a whole.

Patel wasn't close to the people in the same sense that Jawaharlal Nehru was, although Patel dominated the organisation of the Congress while he was alive in a way that Jawaharlal never did. Yet Nehru was the more popular of the two leaders; and hence Gandhi chose him as his successor.... Patel represented what one would call the dominant peasant proprietors of the Indian soil, who came into their own with the national movement, and particularly after 1947, when, on the basis of adult franchise, they became a powerful factor in our polity. There would have been substantial differences in India's development if Patel had lived longer than he did. A lot of the legislation which we enacted in the domain of agrarian reform may have been more muted. Some of the elements of planning for large industry, which we carried out from the mid-fifties onwards, would have acquired a slightly different orientation. In general, the socialist radicalism, which was very active in our country for the last three decades after independence, would have had a much more muted expression.

When Patel died, Nehru felt free to establish what he hoped

would be the guiding principles of independent India. In view of all the violence of partition, it is hardly surprising that one of those principles was secularism. Secularism to Nehru did not mean that religion had to be outlawed; but unlike Gandhi, he did insist that religion and politics be separated. Gandhi had attempted to free religion from formal institutions and priestly hierarchies, rejecting caste prejudice and bigotry. But religion thus purified remained at the centre of his political creed; and secularism for him had meant equal respect for all religions. Nehru, on the other hand, was an avowed agnostic, who believed that religious ritual of any sort had no place in public life. According to Ravindra Kumar, his success in promoting this view in India was limited.

> Nehru's attempt was not only to de-link religion from the formal and vested institutions of religion, but also to push religion to the private domain of operation. Religion was a very valid value for the individual in his personal life, but it should not play or operate upon the political arena. This was a further refinement of the concept of secularism as defined by Gandhi, which Nehru tried to project onto our political scene. Very frankly, I don't think he was successful in this endeavour, for the simple reason that the popular mind in India has really no notion of the distinction between the public and private domain that one is talking of.

Although Nehru succeeded in preventing India's development into a theocratic state like Pakistan, he was unable to banish Hindu revivalism from politics altogether; and in later years, under his successors, it was to play an increasingly ominous role. Hindu revivalism fed, in particular, on the guilt by association which tarred the large minority of Muslims who stayed on in India after partition. A leading Muslim journalist, M. J. Akbar, explains the peculiar dilemma which the existence of Pakistan created for Indian Muslims.

> This sub-continent was partitioned by the Muslims. The guilt of that still remains; the price that has to be paid still remains. The real tragedy is that the price of partition is not being paid by the people who got

Pakistan, but by the Muslims in India.... The memory of a nation divided is a powerful one. It seeps into decisions, sub-consciously or unconsciously some-times. It creates an aura of suspicion around the Indian Muslim; it adds to the argument that the Muslim cannot really be trusted.

Nehru was convinced that the only system of government which could hold so vast and diverse a land together was democracy. He brushed aside arguments that it was unwise to give the vote to India's illiterate masses. His cousin, B. K. Nehru, a distinguished civil servant and former High Commis-sioner in London, doubts the wisdom of this decision.

Under the British, when these institutions were built up, the franchise was very limited. The Constituent Assembly was elected on the basis of a franchise that limited the vote to 14.2 per cent of the population. And now 100 per cent of the adult population has suddenly got the vote. The consequence is that the representa-tives they send to parliament or the state legislatures have no idea of how the British constitution, which we regard as the model for our behaviour, functions, or what the rule of law involves, or what the position of the permanent civil service is in a modern state. All these institutions pre-suppose for their proper func-tioning a knowledge of the assumptions on which they are based. That being lacking, the institutions them-selves get eroded.

Nehru himself certainly showed a deep understanding of and respect for parliamentary government, even when it meant tolerating vitriolic attacks by his opponents. His sister, Mrs Vijayalakshmi Pandit, herself an experienced parliamentar-ian, says that Nehru would be deeply disappointed if he could see the decline in Indian parliamentary standards today.

My brother attached enormous importance to parlia-ment. He didn't miss a day; he was always there, with that red rose in his button-hole. One time, Ram Manohar Lohia[1] got up and said: 'I'm sick and tired of

1 A leader of the Indian Socialist Party and one of Nehru's most outspoken critics.

hearing about the aristocracy of the Nehrus. I know for a fact that Nehru's grandfather was a peon [messenger] at the Mughal court.' The Congress benches were up in arms, shrieking at him. My brother was sitting there; and presently he got up very slowly and said: 'I'd like to thank the Honourable Member for proving what I've been trying to prove, that I'm one of the people.' Dead silence! I've never forgotten that.

Nehru's colleagues and successors may not have shared his enjoyment of the cut and thrust of parliamentary debate; but his faith in democracy has been vindicated by several free elections and two remarkably smooth changes of government through the ballot-box. Despite mass illiteracy, the Indian voter has shown a robust common sense that is quite capable of seeing through the promises of politicians. A typical example is that of a Chief Minister's wife, campaigning in one of the more backward parts of northern India, who was asked by the villagers: 'If you can't provide us with kerosene and cooking oil during an election campaign, what hope have we got when it's all over?' In the same campaign, a labourer digging a canal grumbled: 'Whoever I give my vote to, will put it in his own stomach.' Such cynicism, however, has not made Indians any less enthusiastic about voting: they still love elections. But the politicians are less and less able to take their votes for granted.

Though Nehru was a democrat, he still believed that it was necessary for India to have a strong central government. India did adopt a constitution which was federal in form; but it retained the overriding powers which British viceroys had exercised at the centre. In view of the regional pressures which have been mounting more recently, there are some who argue that a more thorough-going federalism, with more autonomy for the states, would have made for better government and smoother centre-state relations. An eminent constitutional lawyer, L. M. Singhvi, takes this view.

When we framed our constitution, the need for a loose federation had ceased to be; with the creation of Pakistan, the demand for strong provinces had receded. But we did not reckon with the inherent diversities in our country; and we created a strong unitary system in a federal framework. The perception was that India had been historically better off when the central government was strong. That may well be so; but on the other hand, the reality is that the extreme paucity of resources which the states have, and the large responsibilities they are called upon to meet, make it clear that in the very near future India will have to re-define and re-cast its federal equation. It will have to be made more co-operative.

While Nehru insisted on maintaining this centralist bias, he did bow to pressure from the states on the issue of language. He had been reluctant to alter the provincial boundaries left behind by the British, because he realised what a Pandora's Box that would open. But when a politician in Madras fasted to death, demanding a new state in which Telegu[1] would be the official language, Nehru surrendered and accepted the principle of state boundaries defined by language. He said at the time: 'We've disturbed the hornets' nest, and I believe most of us are likely to be badly stung.' He was right; disputes over state boundaries are still raging. Morarji Desai, the stern moralist who later became India's first non-Congress prime minister, argues that instead of surrendering to the clamour for linguistic states, Nehru should have been more whole-hearted about promoting Hindi, the language of northern India, as the national language.

> I told Pandit Jawaharlal Nehru that he was making a great mistake ... because this is a vast country, and it is known as one country in spite of all the different languages, religions and other things. Linguism brings in fanaticism, which is not good. If a common language had been properly done, there would have been no difficulty. English is known only to about four per cent of the people; it can't become a common language, because it's not our own language. And Hindi did not come in as much as it should have done.... They were not very earnest about it from the very beginning. Jawaharlal himself was more a protag-

[1] The language of the Andhra region of the old British province of Madras.

26

onist of English, so what could they do? ... His own whole training was in England; from the age of nine he was educated in England. His father, Pandit Motilal Nehru, was more an Englishman than an Indian; and it's said that he even used to get his clothes washed in Paris!

Certainly, no Parisian laundry could cope with the immaculately white, homespun cotton or *khadi* that Morarji Desai always wears; only an Indian *dhobi* can get the starch to the correct consistency and the creases in the right directions.

Along with religious and linguistic fanaticism, a major obstacle to Nehru's dream of establishing a Western-style democracy on Indian soil was the absence of an effective party system. Mahatma Gandhi had seen Congress as a movement rather than a political party and had advocated that it should be wound up after independence, making way for new parties formed on ideological lines. But Nehru insisted that the survival of Congress was essential at this critical juncture; and he had his way. Unfortunately, the Congress Party let him down badly when it came to implementing the brave new policies to which it was officially committed. After independence, Congressmen exchanged their idealism for the more usual pursuits of politicians – power and its fruits. They found willing allies and accomplices among the bureaucracy they inherited from the Raj. Corruption and nepotism, after all, were not invented in independent India. They had respectable antecedents in the colonial past and before, says Philip Mason, a senior member of the élite imperial civil service and an authoritative historian of the Raj.

There was always corruption in India; it was endemic, and it is bound to be in a poor country. We paid very low wages. But it really arises out of the basic concept of government with which we ran India in the nineteenth century. It was based on the *laissez faire* school of thought, which meant that one left the country to get on with its own personal improvement and provided a framework in which people could live at peace. You kept the taxes as low as possible. Therefore, government servants were paid very little. In fact, every government servant – and the further down the scale you got, the more so – received a great deal more than their actual pay, very often perfectly honestly.

For instance, the *patwari*, the man who kept the village records, was paid ten rupees a month, rising to twelve, and eventually to fourteen after thirty years' service. But his actual income was more like 200 rupees – an honest *patwari*. If he wished to be dishonest, he could probably make more. But the business of the ICS[1] officials was to catch them out when they went over the margin. You had to be very careful not to be so strict that you gummed up the whole works. If you had tried to stop everything, if you'd really been insistent on honesty at the lower level, I don't know what would have happened.

The colonial bureaucracy, with its 'law and order' approach to government, its commitment to the social *status quo*, and its lack of developmental experience, was hardly an ideal instrument for the social and economic transformation which independent India had set as its goal. Nehru and other nationalists had promised often enough in the past to abolish the colonial 'steel-frame' when they came to power. Instead, they soon found themselves working closely with their erstwhile opponents in the services and relying heavily on their advice and assistance. According to Professor Ravindra Kumar, such a compromise was inherent in the nature of India's nationalist movement.

The terms of the Indian revolution, the terms on which India came to be independent in 1947, almost precluded the total transformation of the social order. Dramatic social transformation has been attempted in other major societies like Russia and China, not with the instrumentality of bureaucracy, but much more through party cadres. The structure of the Congress Party itself was such that it was not an appropriate instrument for bringing change in our society; and it was in view of this that Jawaharlal selected the civil

1 The Indian Civil Service, the exclusive senior cadre which ran the Raj.

service as the basis of social change in India. A lot of social scientists would argue that bureaucracies replicate the given power structure in society; they don't transform it. I think there's a very strong point in this; and many problems in India may well flow from this. But one doesn't have free options in a society; one has to work with the instruments that are around.

REVOLUTION BY CONSENT

The 1950s were the golden years of Indian independence, an era of optimism and enlightened leadership, when the country seemed to be carrying through the essential tasks of modernisation at home, while also emerging as the leading international spokesman for the newly independent Third World. The person who seemed to epitomise the spirit of the new India was its prime minister, Pandit Jawaharlal Nehru. In those early years, his government was far from being a one-man band. Many of his Cabinet colleagues and provincial satraps were experienced and capable administrators in their own right, as Professor Ravindra Kumar, Director of the Nehru Museum in Delhi, reminds us.

> There were men of stature, both in New Delhi and in the provincial capitals, who couldn't be lightly pushed aside. They were not the sort of men who would offer challenges to Jawaharlal Nehru's power; but within their own domains or bailiwicks, they would jolly well do what they liked. They were men whose position was quite autonomous, who did not draw their power from Nehru, though they couldn't challenge him.

Although Nehru was never an absolute ruler – and would not have wanted to be – his personal charm and integrity, his intellectual stature and westernised sophistication, did single him out as the public voice of the nation. Taya Zinkin, then *The Guardian*'s correspondent in India, explains the particular appeal he had for Westerners.

Nehru was immensely inspiring. He was not only very good-looking, but he spoke superb English and he was a good writer. Everybody was vaguely in love with him in a platonic sort of way. Even for the hard core of Britishers, he was so much like some of them that they could hand over without feeling that they were ditching the boat; whereas, for example, Morarji Desai[1] would have made a less good impression. What they didn't realise was that, in fact, India owed its survival from partition to two people who were totally different from Nehru. One was Pandit Pant,[2] and the other was Vallabhai Patel, both admirable administrators and ruthless people who understood politics, whereas Nehru was really an idealist. He's been described as the Hamlet of the East, and I think that's right.

Then and later, the most widely held criticism of Nehru was that he vacillated and procrastinated, lacking the single-minded determination that the situation sometimes demanded. Nehru's tentative approach to decision-making, his capacity to see both sides of every argument, was firmly rooted in his eclectic political philosophy. British liberalism and socialism had been the most formative influences during his student years in England; and in some respects, he remained a Fabian of the London School of Economics variety. Later, during the 1930s, he was also much impressed by Marxist theory and by the apparent successes of the Soviet Union under Stalin.

But Nehru was no more dogmatic in politics than in religion. The democratic socialism he tried to establish in India was an attempt to combine the liberalism of the British welfare state with Soviet-style central planning. It was flawed from the outset by the fact that India had neither the revenue nor the administration necessary to run a welfare state, and that Nehru was not prepared to use Stalinist strong-arm tactics to

1 Known for his orthodox Gandhian fads, Desai was Chief Minister of the undivided Bombay state and later served as Nehru's Finance Minister. In the 1970s, he led the opposition to Nehru's daughter, Indira Gandhi, and was Prime Minister of India's first non-Congress government from 1977–79.
2 Another orthodox Gandhian who was Chief Minister of the United Provinces or U.P. (now Uttar Pradesh), India's largest and most populous state.

implement his economic plans. His critics argue that he would have done better to encourage the private initiative and enterprise for which Indian businessmen are so renowned in other parts of the world, including Britain. But Professor Ravindra Kumar points out that unbridled free enterprise was not a realistic option for India.

> We could have developed purely in terms of a society in which property and the profit motive are the basis of social action. There were forces in our society which wanted to move the country along this way, just as there were forces which wanted to establish the social ownership of productive wealth in the country. I think what Jawaharlal did very consciously was to skirt a middle path between these two extremes. Theoretically, it might have been possible to gain a certain measure of economic buoyancy in our country in terms of a pure, free enterprise economy for a short time. But this would also have led to the sort of polarisations of wealth which would have created tremendous social tensions. Already we have a skewed distribution of property ownership in our country, and already we have substantial social conflict flowing from this factor. If this had been permitted to flow unhindered by state policy, I think we would have had disastrous consequences.

The results of Nehru's Fabian socialism were certainly not disastrous. But the jungle of laws, regulations and controls that sprang up in the name of socialism undoubtedly gave it a bad name and provided a happy hunting-ground for corrupt politicians and bureaucrats. One example is that of an Indian industrialist who says there are no less than thirteen government inspectors who can close his factory down. None are apparently interested in inspecting the safety, quality, pollution levels, or whatever else they are supposed to inspect. All that they are interested in is collecting their pay-offs. L. K. Jha, a veteran economic adviser to the government since the 1960s, admits that the system has spawned corruption, but argues that there was no alternative to controls in an economy with serious shortages.

When you have shortages, the tendency to have recourse to rationing for fairer distribution is normal. Initially, capital was short for industry, and so industrial licensing came in. But it was not tight. All you had to do was to see that investments were in industries which were according to the [government's] Plan; the rest was reasonably your own business. But when the shortage of foreign exchange came, then the scrutiny of each case began to get tighter. This process was essentially well-meaning; and each controller saw the rationale of what he was doing – how else could you do without it?

But the system was creating problems – not only too many controls, but too many controllers. Each controller being under a different department meant a different [permanent] secretary, a different minister, and so on. In that system, the room for patronage and corruption increased. It would be taking too Machiavellian a view of the bureaucracy to believe that they invented or perpetuated the system merely because it gave them opportunities for corruption. But when you have a system in which delays are frequent, speed-money is a necessary counterpart.

For all his idealism, Nehru accepted the fact that there was no simple answer to corruption, any more than there was to poverty. But he did have great faith in modern science and technology as the answer to poverty; and as a nationalist, he was determined that India should produce its own scientists. The developed world, he was convinced, would only part with outdated know-how, keeping India permanently backward. Dr M. G. K. Menon, Scientific Adviser to India's present prime minister, is a member of the Royal Society. He describes how Nehru, and later his daughter and political heir, Indira Gandhi, made sure that India entered the space age on its own wings.

At the time India became independent in 1947, we had a very good base in science and some outstanding scientists. But all of them were essentially working in the fields of basic research, as teachers in educational establishments. So we had very little applied science or technology. Jawaharlal Nehru had a very strong intuitive feeling about the role of science and technology for development. And, in the absence of a real base covering the broad spectrum of science and technology, what he did was to support all the very best individuals he had and allow them to build up institutions and areas of capability across a very wide spectrum. That is how we developed the Atomic Energy and Space Programmes, the whole chain of laboratories under the Council of Scientific and Industrial Research, universities, institutes of technology and so on. This was over a longish period, from 1947 until Jawaharlal Nehru passed away in 1964. The period after this was another long period characterised by Indira Gandhi and *her* support for science. Nehru, of course, took a degree from Cambridge in Natural Sciences; Mrs Gandhi didn't; but being with him, she had a very similar feeling about the role of science and technology for development and had strong friendships with many of our great scientists. And she continued the Nehru tradition.

Along with this scientific approach went a strong commitment to expanding India's industrial base. Nehru was much criticised at home and abroad for over-investing in heavy industries like steel and engineering, some of which turned out to be white elephants. But according to Professor Sukhamoy Chakravarty, a leading Indian economist, these new temples of industry were inspired by a legitimate desire to free India from a colonial mode of production, 'characterised very basically by inability to provide the necessary capital goods from within the system itself.' Though many of these new industrial plants were established in the public sector, Professor Chakravarty argues that Nehru had no doctrinaire commitment to state ownership.

Heavy industries require a long period of time to mature, so he thought that the state was in the best possible position to take up investment in those areas directly. But he assigned a very considerable role to the private sector. In the Industrial Policy Resolution of 1956, he made it very clear that he had in mind a mixed economy, with a certain bias in favour of state investment to begin with, which he felt later on could possibly be reduced if the other sectors would come up.

Nehru's critics argue that, if he had not concentrated so much on heavy industry and invested instead in consumer goods like textiles, the Indian economy would have seen more rapid growth of profits and production. But Professor Chakravarty says that Nehru has good reasons for preferring steel to textiles as the basis of India's industrialisation.

His main concern was that a modern textile industry, if it were encouraged too much, would take away a great deal of employment from the handloom sectors. The other aspect that he had in mind was that many of the newly developing countries were coming up with new textile mills, and he feared that there would be a great deal of competition in that particular sector. So he thought of steel. India was well endowed with iron ore and what looked like fairly good reserves of coking coal; it had the natural resource endowment, and also the experience of Tata Steel,[1] to go ahead and emerge as a major producer of steel at fairly low cost. And that, he thought, would trigger off major structural change, which would also be reflected, in the course of time, on the export front, getting from primary exports to industrial manufactured exports.

Nehru's hopes of making India a major exporter of manufactured goods have not been fulfilled. Even so, as Professor Chakravarty points out, his industrial strategy did help to diversify India's exports and produced an industrial structure better equipped to survive the international recession of the 1980s than many other developing economies in Latin America and Africa.

The main weakness in Nehru's economic planning lay, not in his industrial priorities, but in his neglect of agriculture, on

1 India's first steel plant, established in colonial times by J. N. Tata, founder of the country's largest and most advanced industrial empire.

36

which the vast majority of Indians continued to depend for their employment and subsistence. Professor Chakravarty believes that the real neglect here was in implementation rather than in policy.

> Nehru expected agriculture to function as a bargain sector, so that very little investment would produce very high results, which I'm afraid was an utterly optimistic projection of the possibilities of growth in Indian agriculture. For a while, it didn't really matter very much, because there was a considerable amount of unutilised land which could be brought into cultivation; so the production growth rate was reasonable. But by the eary 1960s, it had really run out of steam. We were not really prepared for changing the technological basis of Indian agriculture until the droughts came in the sixties.

When it became clear that there was little room for growth through expanding the area under cultivation, the Government finally woke up to the fact that productivity had to be increased through new technology. One reason why this awareness was so late in coming was that an essential element of Nehru's reform programme had remained unimplemented. This was the introduction of cooperative farming to replace the large feudal estates which had been abolished by law. Another distinguished economist, Dr C. T. Kurien of the Institute of Development Studies in Madras, attributes this omission to Nehru's lack of grit when it came to implementing unpopular changes.

> Nehru was not as determined as his vision had called for; and the most clear example was the resolution of the Congress Party in 1959 to go in for cooperativisation of land. Cooperative cultivation was not compelled collectivisation, but an attempt to bring together [small] farmers to work as one larger unit in the midst of all the petty landholdings one was confronting. But there was such big opposition to it from the larger landlords, and from political forces within the Congress Party, that Nehru just withdrew. Much

stronger commitment to action was called for; but that was not to be seen.

Despite such shortcomings, by the late 1950s Nehru appeared to have set India on a course of peaceful, democratic reform. Taya Zinkin of *The Guardian* had her own reservations about the statist aspects of Indian planning, but her overall impression was positive.

> It was change by consensus. One of the big reforms was the reform of Hindu law, which was an electoral issue and rightly so, because it could have aroused a lot of antagonism from a very orthodox electorate. Nehru did everything in a democratic way. There were no purges; there was no revolution; there was no witch-hunting either. One wasn't totally with him, because of various economic idiosyncracies which didn't make much sense. But on the whole, he had a good package.

Nehru also dreamt of leading a revolution in world affairs. He wanted the voice of the poorer nations to be heard for the first time and was not prepared to be fobbed off by mere verbal diplomacy from the rich countries, such as changing India's designation from a 'backward' to a 'developing' nation. Even Winston Churchill, who had opposed Indian independence till the end, eventually came to recognise Nehru's pre-eminence in the Third World, describing him as 'The Light of Asia'.

It was Nehru who resisted Anglo-American pressure and insisted that China be allowed to attend the Bandung Conference of 1955, the forerunner of what was to be the world non-aligned movement. At a time when the West still treated Red China as a pariah, it was Nehru who argued forcefully that it was lunacy to try and isolate or encircle one of the world's largest and most populous states. He believed that the two giants of Asia must stand together if the continent was to be free of the economic and political domination of the two great power blocs. But that was not to be. Within a year of Bandung, Nehru was receiving reports that Chinese caravans were passing through a north-western border area known as Aksai Chin, a bleak no-man's-land which India claimed on the basis of the colonial boundaries imposed by the Raj. When talks with the Chinese leadership got him nowhere, Nehru gave in to pressure from the more chauvinistic sections of Indian public opinion and agreed to what was known as the Forward Policy. This involved moving Indian security forces further into the disputed area, even at the risk of clashes with Chinese border posts. General Vohra was at the time the senior officer responsible for planning India's defences on its eastern border with China. He argues that the Forward Policy provoked the Chinese into a war for which India was not prepared.

> The Indian Army had no training or equipment for high-altitude warfare. These areas are all snowbound, and you need special equipment, special types of clothing, special logistical arrangements to be able to support operations in this area. Secondly, the Indian army, which was about two million strong during the Second World War, was being drastically cut down. If I remember correctly, the size of the Indian army in the early sixties was only 500 000; so you can see that we were not at all thinking of manning the northern border effectively.
>
> If the Government felt that a war was inevitable with the Chinese over the Aksai Chin issue, then the wiser thing would have been to play for time to organise and equip our forces and then issue the ultimatum. To my mind, it was purely a political decision and it was against professional advice. The idea was that we should show our flag right up to the border. That is good as far as it goes; but what it does not cater for is that, should the showing of the flag lead to skirmishes or even to a major conflict, are you trained, equipped and prepared for it? So the Forward Policy should have been a cautious policy, not a policy which permitted an escalation. I therefore call it a political débâcle, not a military débâcle.

A factor which further demoralised India's armed forces was the erratic and irascible personality of Nehru's close friend and Defence Minister, V. K. Krishna Menon. General K. P. Candeth worked closely with Menon in those days. 'His manners were such,' he complains, 'that he upset nearly everybody who dealt with him. He was very rude and abrupt; and his manner of working was such that neither the ordinary soldier nor the army officer could understand it.' Menon used to work through the night, and his habit of calling people up in the early hours caused particular annoyance. 'Most army officers had gone to sleep or they'd had a party,' Candeth chuckles. 'They didn't appreciate being asked to give their views at 2 o'clock in the morning, especially when there wasn't a war. I mean, why couldn't it wait till the morning?'

In the border war that followed, the Chinese defeated the Fourth Indian Division, which had been described as 'incomparable' by Field-Marshal Slim during the Second World War. But with the tea-gardens of Assam at their feet, the victors suddenly announced a unilateral ceasefire and withdrew to the disputed border. They had inflicted a humiliating punishment on India; and one of their leaders, Liu Xiaoqi, boasted that India's arrogance and delusions of grandeur had been destroyed.

For Nehru, an equally bitter pill to swallow was his party's insistence that he sack Krishna Menon, who had always been seen as his personal protégé. Another close confidante of Nehru's in those days was his sister, Vijayalakshmi Pandit, renowned for her beauty and her imperious ways in various top diplomatic posts, including that of High Commissioner in London. She explains why her brother was so close to Menon: 'To whom could my brother go to and talk? All his other ministers were on a different level from himself; but Krishna Menon had the same background and they talked the same language.'

Mrs Pandit complains that, on the subject of relations with China, Menon was less than entirely honest with his patron.

> Krishna Menon wasn't always straight with him. There were lots of things he knew which he didn't pass on to my brother. And that is the biggest blow my brother had …, when the Cabinet gave him the choice of resigning or getting Krishna to resign. He was absolutely stunned by it, because he'd put all his trust in Krishna Menon. That was his way; if he trusted you, he trusted you absolutely; there were no half-

measures. And when finally Krishna Menon had to go, it upset him a lot.

According to Mrs Pandit, Nehru's personal disillusionment with Krishna Menon was mirrored by his larger sense of betrayal by the Chinese, who had shattered his vision of Asian cooperation. Nehru's faithful private secretary, N. K. Seshan, confirms what a shock this was.

> I don't think he ever believed, even for a moment, that China would attack India. There might be border skirmishes; but he was aware that the army was not in a position, if attacked, to send the Chinese back. It was only for public consumption that he said: 'I have ordered the army to throw the Chinese out'. There was nothing else that he could do.

Although Nehru clearly misread Chinese intentions on the border issue, few people today would doubt the wisdom of his long-term assessment that the world must come to terms with Communist China. And despite the collapse of his China policy, Nehru's friendship with the rest of the Communist world has proved an enduring legacy both to India and the non-aligned movement. He was the architect of that special relationship with the Soviet Union which remains a cornerstone of India's foreign policy today. His critics at home and abroad often attacked him for being too 'soft' on Moscow, and especially for not condemning the Russian invasion of Hungary in 1956. But Nehru was certainly no Soviet stooge, still less an uncritical admirer of Communism. His friendship with Moscow followed partly from the repugnance he felt for the materialism and the McCarthyite cold war mentality of the West, and partly from a pragmatic assessment of India's interests.

A. P. Venkateswaran, till recently a senior diplomat who served as India's Foreign Secretary,[1] argues that Nehru's non-alignment was not an idealistic pose but a realistic attempt to extend Indian independence into the international arena.

---

1   In India, a Secretary to Government is the senior civil servant in charge of a department.

The basic aim of non-alignment was to strengthen the independence of decision-making among the newly independent countries, and that you could achieve only by being yourself and not belonging to any power bloc. The moment you belong to a power bloc, you have to vote with them, whichever way it goes; whereas non-alignment meant that you took decisions on the merits of each case, in consonance with your own national interests.

Although India wished to remain non-aligned, in this sense of preserving its freedom of manoeuvre, it clearly needed outside sources of industrial and military aid and know-how to build up its own capacity in these areas. At a time when the West tended to treat those who were not with them as against them, Nehru found Moscow far more obliging in making such aid available without strings. Inder Gujral, later India's ambassador in Russia, stresses that Nehru first turned to the Soviets for arms because the West turned him down.

To a considerable extent, Indo-Soviet relations have grown because of the West's policies. Before the China War, India never did any arms shopping in the Soviet Union. We were all the time buying either from the British or the Americans. It was only after 1962, when we wanted to modernise the Indian army, that we felt we had to do something. Chavan, who was Defence Minister under Jawaharlal Nehru, was asked to go first to London and then to Washington to request two second-hand submarines. I emphasise second-hand, because we didn't have a submarine till then. He came back with a blank; both refused. And then, for the first time, he was sent to Moscow.

Chavan's mission to Moscow was cut short abruptly by Nehru's death in May 1964. Those who were close to the Prime Minister in his final years, say that his spirit and his health had never really recovered from the China War. 'He was a different Nehru after the Chinese attack,' says N. K. Seshan. 'It was not the same Nehru I had known before. You sometimes used to get the feeling when you'd go to him that he was lost; that he wasn't taking any notice of what you were telling him. I had never seen him broken before through the many crises he had faced; but this one really broke him.'

The acid test for Seshan was that the Prime Minister, who had always insisted on drafting his own letters and public statements, now never bothered to amend any draft put up to him. 'He would just initial every one of them,' recalls Seshan. 'He had no interest at all in life.'

In January 1964, Nehru suffered a mild stroke; but he showed that his spirit was not entirely broken by spurning his doctors' advice to convalesce. 'Let them go to hell,' he said. 'If I lie down for even a week, I know I'll not get up.' Four months later, India's first prime minister died in harness. His official biographer, Dr S. Gopal, suggests that he died as a prophet frustrated, with his hopes unfulfilled. Not all his hopes were frustrated; but his revolution by consent had suffered a severe setback from the China débâcle and many of his reforms had been tied up in a bureaucratic tangle.

THE
NETA-BABU RAJ

There is no better commentator on modern India than the *Times of India* cartoonist, R. K. Laxman. He has three regular characters: a politician, an apparently sycophantic bureaucrat and an old man watching their antics with bemused amusement. According to Laxman, the old man represents 'the man who stands in the queue, the man who shares all the miseries of India, the victim of the politicians and the bureaucrats.'

'Conditions are pretty bad, Sir – Unless you take in a couple of more "Yes" men to help, the situation is going to be tough!'

Laxman makes no apology for doing what Western corre-
spondents are always accused of doing – presenting a negative
image of India. 'Democracy,' he says, 'demands a cartoonist.
The first victim of dictatorship is a cartoonist, as happened
during the Emergency [1975–77] here in India. I don't think the
function of a cartoonist is to promote, but to destroy, to carp,
to criticise. It is a destructive art, nevertheless a very essential
one for democracy.'

Political cartoons must reflect real life otherwise they have
no relevance. The success of Laxman indicates how close he
does get to real life. He concentrates on the conflict between
the politician and the bureaucrat on the one side and the
common man on the other. So central is that conflict to the life
of India that some economists have coined the phrase 'Neta
[Politician] Babu [Bureaucrat] Raj' to describe the political
economy. The Netas and the Babus manipulate the complicated socialist controls set up by Jawaharlal Nehru to their
advantage and to the advantage of their clients: contractors,
traders, businessmen, and larger farmers. Prem Shankar Jha,
an economist and journalist who has written a book on the
Neta-Babu Raj, describes the people in whose interest it
operates.

> Slow economic growth in India after 1965 was not
> caused by the two sudden droughts we had, or by the
> war with Pakistan, or by sudden overspending, or even
> by the wrong growth strategy. Slow growth was
> caused by political changes which brought into power
> a class that had a strong vested interest in a regime of
> perpetual shortages of everything. It is a class of people
> who are broadly speaking self-employed; all those
> who are able to retain or increase their real incomes in
> the face of inflation. Typically they are the self-em-
> ployed, because traders, lawyers, doctors, managers of
> industry and to some extent artisans are able to charge
> cost plus. Among them, I would say the two groups
> with real muscle are the trading classes and the owner-
> managers of capital who have come into being as a
> result of planning and forced economic development
> after independence.

How then is this class linked to the politicians and bureau-

46

crats? Prem Shankar Jha believes there is an obvious link: 'This class over a period of time converted its economic power into political power by financing elections. Then the politicians in their turn bent the bureaucracy to their will.'

The theory is that under the Neta-Babu Raj, traders and industrialists make their profits by pushing up prices and selling on the black market, rather than by increasing production or improving the quality of what they make. They have, therefore, a vested interest in shortages which automatically push up prices and create a black market. The traders and industrialists have found natural allies among the larger farmers who have benefited from India's green or agricultural revolution. Dr C. T. Kurien of the Institute of Development Studies in Madras explains why it is only the larger farmers who have been able to benefit from the Green Revolution.

> In the interests of increased food production in this country, there was a large-scale subsidising of digging tubewells and installing pumps. Now, in itself getting water from the depth of the earth is a good thing and certainly helpful for agriculture, but it is only possible for those who can afford it to go in for tubewells.

Dr Kurien points out that, after getting help from the Government to dig their tubewells, the larger farmers turn from growing the food-grain that the poor need to more profitable cash crops. The farm lobby is interested in getting Government to peg food prices artificially high, not in increasing the supply of food. The new farmers use tractors, tubewells and chemical fertilisers but they are as rapacious as the old feudal landlords they replaced and lack the paternalism which was the one redeeming feature of some of the Indian feudals.

George Fernandes is a socialist politician who served as Industries Minister in the short-lived Janata Government which came to power after Mrs Gandhi's only electoral defeat in 1977. He believes that the Neta-Babu Raj has evolved because independent India did not destroy the old élite left behind by the British Raj.

> This establishment has the upper castes of India. It has the money-bags of India too, the industrialists who

have their international linkages. This establishment also has the English-knowing élite of India. So you have caste, you have money, and you have English, a language of exploitation in India, a language which is used to instil a feeling of inferiority in the overwhelming mass of people, making them totally irrelevant to the whole democratic process. This threesome is the bane of our national situation today.

George Fernandes goes on to make an extreme claim:

I don't think the British have had better allies than the Government in Delhi in terms of perpetuating what was going on. I think things have reached a point where the older generation in the rural areas say we were better off forty years ago. It hurts me to even mention this.

George Fernandes is a politician, and they deal in hyperbole. Few people in India would take as dismal a view of the forty years since independence as he does. There is a lot to be said for continuity, as other developing countries which have destroyed their élites have found. The apogee of the English-speaking élite left behind by the British Raj are the members of the Indian Civil Service (ICS). They have served independent India with great distinction. B. K. Nehru is one of them. A cousin of Jawaharlal Nehru, he has held many senior positions since independence including the governorships of Kashmir and Assam at very sensitive times. He was also High Commissioner in London during the Emergency. B. K. Nehru has no doubt that the continuity his cousin preserved was right for India. 'I may be prejudiced,' he says, 'because I belong to the ICS. But I think one of the most valuable things the British left behind was the senior administrative services and the tradition of these services.'

But these traditions have been undermined by the Neta-Babu Raj. The ICS officer of the Raj did not have to cope with all-powerful politicians. His loyalty was to his service and he knew that the traditions of that service would protect him from the limited political pressures he might come up against during the latter days of British rule. The modern Indian civil servant does not enjoy that protection. The fight between the civil servant and the politician is very unequal, as B. K. Nehru explains.

> The civil servant is supposed to administer the law, and not the whims or orders or wishes of the Minister. Now if the Minister wants him to forget the law and to do what he wants to be done irrespective of the law, the correct thing for the civil servant to do is to refuse. All right, some do. There are very honourable exceptions who have throughout suffered the consequences. Suspension, denial of promotion and transfer are the three powers that have been used to bend civil servants to the Minister's will. What does a married man with children do if he's told to do something and says 'I won't'? So the next day he finds himself transferred. Now his children can't get admission to schools, he can't get a house; it causes complete dislocation to his life. So it's not surprising that so many have succumbed to these pressures.

The esprit de corps of the civil service has been undermined by these pressures, and civil servants have become politicians' 'most obedient servants'. When young men and women enter the civil service, they are competent, correct and enthusiastic. Unfortunately, they do not get the support they need from their disillusioned seniors. In many district offices, the British tradition of painting the names of previous collectors or magistrates or superintendents of police on boards is preserved. Those boards show how quick the turnover is nowadays. The reason which young officers in the districts always give for this is that their predecessors have fallen foul of the local politicians. If their seniors in the headquarters of the State Governments stood by them, they would be able to resist the political pressures. All too often, the senior members of government services do not resist the politicians' demands to transfer uncooperative officers.

Morarji Desai, the man who became India's first non-Congress Prime Minister, has always compaigned vigorously for administrative propriety. During his long career he has been more of a preacher than a politician. He believes that the basis of sound administration is a civil servant who stands up to politicians when they are asked to bend the law. 'There are very few public servants now,' he complains, 'who will oppose a wrong order.' Never one to doubt his own rectitude, Morarji Desai proudly asserts: 'I started my life as a member of a public service in the British government. I never carried out an order which I considered wrong. If they dismissed me, I was prepared to be dismissed, but they could not do that because I was right and they were wrong.'

Sadly for Morarji, in spite of the rectitude he so publicly proclaimed, during his prime ministership there were damaging allegations against his son, Kanti. Morarji could never bring himself to throw Kanti out of the Prime Minister's house, a gesture which would have silenced his critics. It would also have ended any influence that Kanti might have been peddling.

The development economist, Dr C. T. Kurien, believes that the problem is much more complicated than simply reviving the tradition of not obeying illegal orders. He feels that Nehru should have cut the bureaucracy down to size.

> Nehru had a wonderful opportunity to build up institutions which would have demonstrated very clearly that the bureaucracy he inherited was to be only a limited instrument and not to become substantially the agency that determines the priorities of people. The popular involvement in the freedom struggle had just ended. That involvement could have and should have been canalised to build up institutions at the lower level, where there could have been much more interaction between the ordinary people and the business-making and implementing machinery.

Nehru was not much interested in administration and institutions. Lord Louis Mountbatten, India's last Viceroy and first Governor-General, was. He left Nehru a list of administrative 'do's' and 'don'ts' including one about salaries: 'Corruption and nepotism – this is on the increase. The undue lowering of the standard of living among the higher wage groups is likely to lead to a lowering of their normal standards of probity.' Nehru ignored that warning; and Mountbatten's words

proved all too prophetic. Prem Shankar Jha even goes so far as
to suggest that politicians have deliberately kept civil servants'
salaries down so that they are tempted to be corrupt.

> I don't think it is accidental that the salaries of civil
> servants went down in money terms between 1947 and
> 1977; for thirty years it actually went down. In real
> terms, the real income of the senior bureaucrats went
> down to about 20 per cent of what it used to be, and
> living became impossible. You had a choice: you either
> joined your minister and you made a profit and got
> rapid promotions; or you didn't join your minister and
> you were out in the street.

There are many economists who do not go along with Prem
Shankar Jha's theory that there has been a conspiracy by the
Netas, the Babus and their clients to hold the commanding
heights of the Indian economy. One is the distinguished economist, Professor Sukhamoy Chakravarty.

> I don't believe any conspiratorial theory of history, so I
> certainly don't think there has been a plot to create an
> economy of shortages in this country, to give the
> bureaucrats and politicians power by controlling and
> managing shortages. But there are such things as unin-
> tended outcomes; this is a well established sociological
> law. Some of the things which are done, such as the
> regulatory frameworks with a view to conserve foreign
> exchange and many other scarce materials, have
> turned out to be fetters. We should re-examine those
> controls and try to open up these areas for productive
> forces.

In spite of the Neta-Babu Raj, the Indian economy has grown
steadily without the runaway inflation or indebtedness that
has characterised so many developing countries. There are,
however, economists who argue that bureaucratic India has
been too cautious, that it should have gone for a higher
growth-rate at the risk of inflation and of not being able to
meet its international debts. Professor Chakravarty does not
agree.

I do not really like gambling, and I feel that the lessons we can draw from the experiences of Latin America and Africa should make us much more cautious about such a strategy, particularly when the world growth-rate and the growth of trade is fairly low. There is absolutely no sign of its gaining the momentum it acquired in the late fifties and sixties. That sort of situation is much more conducive to taking risks. In a situation in which world trade itself is growing very slowly, to take a market from other countries which are struggling to survive is a very difficult proposition.

The economist and civil servant, L. K. Jha, was asked by Mrs Gandhi to head a committee to look into ways of cutting back the jungle of red tape strangling initiative in India. He did not get very far and blames the lack of reliable international 'life-belts' for countries which get into economic difficulties. Nevertheless, he is not sure whether India has been right to play so safe in its international borrowings. 'I sometimes ask myself,' he muses, 'whether some future historian will say it was better to have borrowed and defaulted than not to have borrowed enough.'

A start was made towards liberalising the economy under Morarji Desai's Janata Government; but Morarji Desai did not survive long enough as Prime Minister to make a lasting impression. When Rajiv Gandhi came to power, he announced the first all-out assault on India's bureaucratic traditions, but he too has not found the going easy. Within five months of coming to power, he was having to assure his own party that he was not abandoning socialism. He told the All India Congress Committee in Delhi that there was no question of 'wavering from socialism' and 'abandoning' the public sector. He also said there would be no change in the 'time-proven and nationally accepted' policies towards foreign investment and multinational companies. He had to give those assurances because Congressmen were worried that his enthusiasm for economic liberalisation would mean the end of the Neta-Babu Raj which had looked after them so well. So far, he has not made major changes in Indian socialism.

In spite of the Neta-Babu Raj, India has managed to build up an impressive industrial base since independence. It is reckoned by some economists to be the world's tenth largest industrial power, making everything from toothpaste to telecommunications equipment, from aspirins to aeroplanes. Kartik Narayan is an industrialist who remains loyal to the British motor industry when all about him are falling for Japan. He used to make the Standard Herald under licence, and is now producing Rovers for the Indian market, while also making spare parts for London cabs. He believes that, without controls and protection, India would never have been able to build up its industrial base. 'Controls is of course a dirty word,' he says, 'but then, on the other hand, controls have also given the Indian industrialist a certain amount of protection. He has a vast domestic market to cater to and, had this protection not been there, the industrial base would not have been created.' According to Narayan, the limited relaxation of controls which has taken place has allowed companies to grow more naturally, and some are even beginning to enjoy the benefits of the economy of scale. He expects, for instance, that India will probably become the second largest manufacturer of scooters or motorcycles in the world very shortly.

Kartik Narayan is an industrialist in the private sector. Inevitably Nehru's socialism led to the creation of a very large nationalised sector too. This is often described as the 'white elephant' of the Indian economy. Finance Minister after Finance Minister presenting the annual budget has bemoaned the fact that the nationalised industries do not swell his coffers by giving an adequate return on investment. Efficiency and productivity are low in many nationalised industries. One reason for this is political interference, as Professor Chakravarty explains: 'As an economist I feel that there has been too much interfering in the functioning of the public sector by the government. The government should lay down the broad goals and strategies, and the public sector should have been allowed to function much more independently of the day-to-day pressures of the government.' What are those pressures? Bureaucrats fighting over who should have the best positions in managements, politicans demanding jobs for their boys, politically influential contractors pressing claims for their tenders to be accepted, and all the usual goings-on associated with the Neta-Babu Raj.

There are of course some healthy public sector undertakings in India; and one, according to Dr Kurien, is the railways. 'Railways,' he says, 'have on the whole done a very good job. I don't believe that any private enterprise has been able to do the kind of thing that Indian Railways have done.' That, not surprisingly, is also the view of the Railway Minister, Madhav Rao Scindia. He is the head of the royal family of Gwalior, one of the largest of the former princely states, and is the very model of a modern maharaja. He has acquired a considerable knowledge of railway technology and even succeeded in running the railways at a profit, while at the same time subsidising some freight and passenger services. Figures trip off his tongue: '8–9000 kilometres of new routes added since independence'; '580 kilometres electrified in one year'; '4000–4100 kilometres of track renewed each year'; '11 million passengers carried every day'; '300 million tons of freight carried every year'.

In India, the age of the train has never gone. The twenty-two-carriage Grand Trunk Express, double-headed by two Indian-made diesel engines, thunders daily from Delhi in the north to Madras, the capital of the south. At the same time, ancient steam-engines still chug down branch lines which would have been axed if India had ever had the misfortune to have suffered a Dr Beeching. One-hundred-year-old, narrow-gauge engines still huff and puff their way up the hill from Siliguri to Darjeeling. The train takes four times as long as the bus, but then the railways are not over-zealous about collecting fares. So the old Darjeeling Himalayan Railway is still an attractive proposition for genuine passengers with more time than money, not just a relic preserved for tourists.

The railways once again show India's talent for developing the modern without destroying the ancient. The minister, in the midst of all his difficulties in planning bigger and better trains that go faster and further, has still found time to think about the future of steam. 'In the process of modernisation,' he chuckles, 'I'm very clear in my mind that steam does have a future; but the future of steam is entirely limited to our museums. That is the only future of steam.' Nevertheless, he still estimates that there will be steam on Indian railways up to the end of this century; so it will survive a lot longer than on most other major railway systems.

As steam gradually fades out, nuclear energy takes over,

one of several fields in which Indian scientists are among the world's leaders. Dr M. G. K. Menon, scientific adviser to India's present Prime Minister, Rajiv Gandhi, explains the importance for India of nuclear energy.

India has very large reserves of coal, but expressed in *per capita* terms they are not high. A very large part of India is also far away from the coalfields. Therefore, if you base yourself on coal-fired thermal stations, you have to carry coal for them over long distances, which means heavy overheads on transport. Nuclear power does not call for these overheads on transport. The other point is that we have uranium deposits; and even more, we are fairly unique in that, along with Brazil, we have large deposits of thorium.

India's thorium deposits mean that it could eventually have an almost infinite source of nuclear fuel. The next stage for India is to build fast-breeder nuclear reactors. A fast-breeder test reactor has already been built in Madras. From there Dr Menon says India will be able to go on and convert thorium into uranium; but he admits that even Indian science has not managed to escape from the baleful influence of the bureaucracy.

In his last speech, Homi Bhabha[1] made a very pointed reference to the fact that there are many who assume we are very good at administration and that what we lack is science and technology. What he had to say is: 'Yes, we have good administration of the static type, but not of the type required for the innovative changes development calls for.'

L. K. Jha agrees that the Indian administration is clearly constipated and has not broken the mould set by the British.

In the British days, clerks were much cheaper than officers, and you had top graduates, first-class minds, coming and working as clerks for want of anything better to do. The clerks did a lot of work, and a few

[1] The young scientist who pioneered nuclear sciences in India. Bhabha died in an air crash on Mont Blanc.

officers could supervise that work and get the job done. Now the quality of clerks has deteriorated, the better students get so many other opportunities, but the pyramid structure of the bureaucracy remains and you can't change it. The peons [messengers], the clerks, and the umpteen levels remain, because you will either have to sack people, which is ruled out, or at least stop recruitment, which will again create a kind of uproar. There are now bans against the creation of new posts, against fresh recruitment, but their impact will only be felt in ten years, because the number of people retiring each year is relatively small.

British visitors to India who complain to obstructive clerks are often told: 'You taught us bureaucracy.' That may be so; but forty years after independence, it is a rather lame excuse. Surely by now the abominable 'no-man', as one Indian journalist recently described the Indian *Babu*, should be an extinct species. But then all old habits die hard in India, even down to the cynical humour left behind by the British upper middle classes. Take this prayer still hanging in the house of a senior member of the Indian Administrative Service. It reads like something from a British public school magazine:

Oh Lord grant that this day we come to no decisions,
Neither run into any kind of responsibility,
But that all our doings may be ordered to establish
New and quite unwarranted departments.
O Thou who seest all things below
Grant Thy servants may go slow,
That they may study to comply
With regulations till they die.
Teach us Lord to reverence
Committees more than common sense.
Impress our minds to make no plan
But pass the baby when we can.
And when temper seems to give
Us feelings of initiative,
Or when alone we go too far,
Chastise us with a circular.
Mid war and tumult, fire and storms,

Strengthen us we pray with forms.
Thus will Thy servants ever be
A perfect flock of sheep for Thee.

There are some Indian civil servants who do not blame the British legacy for the tardiness and inefficiency of the Indian bureaucracy. One of them is Badrinath Chaturvedi, who has worked for the government of the southern state of Tamil Nadu for many years. He points out that what we in the West regard as efficiency pales into insignificance in Hinduism's cosmic view of the universe.

> The attitude to time in India was that time and space, although two co-ordinates in which human life is placed, do not exhaust human possibilities. Time is not a pragmatic, realistic, physical thing, which can be measured, which governs our lives; it wasn't that at all. Hindus had a concept of time which was immense. If you see the Indian myths, the time is often in terms of millions of years. So if you are five minutes late, it simply does not matter.

Unfortunately, time does seem to matter nowadays. The Indian agricultural scientists, for instance, who led the Green Revolution, had to measure the distance between seed-time and harvest in some way or other, otherwise they would not have achieved the outstanding feat of boosting India's annual food production by one hundred million tons in the last twenty years. It is a massive achievement, but it is still not enough to satisfy India's ever-expanding appetite. According to Dr Kurien, the self-sufficiency in food-grains that Indian officials talk about is not a true measure of whether there is enough food to go round. 'Self-sufficiency in that context,' he says, 'simply means that we are not importing any more. Even by official recognition, 35 to 40 per cent of the people do not have adequate food. So when they say that the country is self-sufficient, it is a very deceptive macro-perception of the situation, looking at it in terms of imports and exports.'

The *per capita* consumption of food-grains is just one more economic indicator showing that Nehru's revolution by consent has been a revolution from the top down, not from the bottom upwards. India still has to find a way to push development down into the huts of the landless labourers and the shacks of the slum-dwellers.

THE BOTTOM OF THE PILE

No problem in India is easy to solve. That is not surprising, because India is facing a task no nation has set itself before – the task of bringing some three hundred million people, some 40 per cent of its population, out of dire poverty without resort to force or compulsion, communism or tyranny. Nehru believed that an industrial revolution would provide the answer to poverty. A revolution there has certainly been. The value of industrial production has risen from six hundred million dollars at independence to 46 billion dollars now. Nehru hoped that socialism would regulate this revolution, preventing the rich getting richer and the poor getting poorer. But as Professor Chakravarty admits, socialist controls have not led to an even distribution of the fruits of growth.

> Twenty to thirty per cent of the population have appropriated the largest part of the gains. Seventy per cent may have shared in it, but very unequally; so much so that you might as well say that forty per cent has not practically been touched, compared with where they were twenty or twenty-five years ago. This aspect of distribution needs much better emphasis, and that cannot be implemented unless we really bring in people down below and involve them in the process of planning.

Although the distribution has been uneven, the money has not all gone into the pockets of the rich. Thirty per cent of India's population is a huge number of people. A vast, new, comparatively affluent middle class has been born. It's those at the bottom of the pile who have been left out by the Neta-Babu Raj. Nowhere is the grip of the Neta-Babu Raj tighter than in the state of Bihar. Set in the middle of the fertile plain of the Ganges, with enormous resources of underground water, coal and minerals, Bihar should be one of India's richest states. In fact it is a byword for backwardness, bureaucratic inertia and corruption. In the small town of Pali in central Bihar, the garden of the Government Rest House has been taken over by about sixty families, all *Harijans* or Untouchables. They have created a small village of their own, consisting of mud huts with doors barely two foot six high. Most of the children are naked and the adults wear torn *lungis* or loin-cloths. They have little to do and less to eat. On the many days when there is no agricultural work available, they are reduced to eating snails. French snails may be a delicacy, Indian ones certainly are not.

All the *Harijan* families did have homes of their own and fairly regular work in the village of Akbarpur, about seven miles away. Some years ago, however, the sons of two farmers belonging to the dominant *Bhumihar* caste were murdered in Akbarpur. The *sarpanch* or village headman called in the police and asked them to charge the *Harijans* with murder. The police officer suggested that it would be simpler to burn down the *Harijans'* houses and drive them out of the village. That is how those families came to be squatting on the lawns of the Government Rest House in Pali. Fourteen *Harijans* have been arrested in connection with the murders. No member of the *Bhumihar* caste has been arrested for setting fire to their huts. The trouble all started because the *Harijans* were refusing to work in the *Bhumihars'* fields unless they were paid the minimum wages laid down by the government. The local officials in Bihar do not enforce the Minimum Wages Act because they are in collusion with the dominant farming caste.

At one stage the scandal of the *Harijans* of Akbarpur did reach the ears of the central government in Delhi. After much to-ing and fro-ing of files, the government of Bihar was persuaded to rebuild the *Harijans'* homes and re-settle them in their own village. The Public Works Department took the building materials to Akbarpur and asked the local police station to guard them. Unfortunately the officer in charge of the police station was a member of a farming caste too. As soon as the Public Works officials had left, he withdrew the police guard, and the farmers sold off the building materials. After that, no further attempt was made to resolve the *Harijans'* problem.

Many *Harijans* and other landless labourers no longer take this collusion between officials and politically influential castes lying down. There are several political groups, outside the main parties, who are working for the long-overdue implementation of the Minimum Wages Act, land reforms and other legislation intended to benefit the landless. These groups motivate the landless to fight for their rights. The farmers, not surprisingly, do not like this. The result has been a series of clashes between the landless and the farmers and some gruesome massacres.

In some areas of Bihar, farmers have recruited private armies to keep down the landless peasants. Not surprisingly it is very rare for a police officer to take a stand against these illegal armies. The Calcutta *Statesman*, in an editorial on the recent murder of *Harijans* by farmers of the *Yadav* caste, wrote:

> In a state where brutal killings have become commonplace, and are accepted as such by both the people and the Government, the recent murder of six *Harijans* by a *Yadav* landlord's musclemen is unlikely to create much of a ripple. In fact, an average of forty people are killed every week in Bihar, either for political or personal reasons. The Bihar Government has taken the seemingly positive step of ordering an enquiry into agrarian tensions, at the same time announcing its decision to enforce existing ceilings on land holdings and introduce new reforms. But no measures have been enforced or initiated since then, while the outcome of the enquiry remains a mystery. This is not at all surprising, since nearly all the Bihar Ministers in charge of important portfolios are themselves big landlords.

The Indian press always talks of 'big landlords', as though the battles taking place in Bihar are essentially feudal. In fact, in central Bihar, the most tense area, the struggle is between farmers with comparatively modest holdings, say thirty acres, and the landless. In central Bihar, the landless are still paid in kind, in spite of a law prescribing a minimum daily cash wage.

Ela Bhatt is a social worker who has spent many years campaigning to improve the conditions of women casual labourers. She attempted to enforce the payment of minimum wages to agricultural workers.

> We went like typical trade unionists in a procession and demanded the minimum wage. The employer organised himself with the other employers. Then we went to the Labour Commissioner. He said: 'Yes they must have the minimum wage.' So a whole party of labour officers came to the village and forced the farmers to give the minimum wage. On that night, of course, all the farmers were very angry. So they got organised, and they called the police under some pretext or other. That was harvest time, so in the middle of the night all the workers were working in the fields. It was then that the police party came, and they [the workers] were beaten up. I also went to the fields and found the police party. I had an argument with the police, and because it was dark they couldn't recognise me, so I also got a *danda* [stave] on my back.

Ela Bhatt then came to realise that, unless she could live in the village, direct confrontation with the farmers would not work; so she tried another approach. The root problem, she felt, was that there was surplus labour. Even if the landless labourers did stick to their demand for their legal rights, there would always be others prepared to accept whatever the farmers offered. So she attempted to increase employment opportunities.

> Today after many years, we have a situation so that families where we are working have three sources of income. One is their traditional employment. Secondly we have tried to revive their home-based crafts, like weaving, pottery, carpentry and other things. The third source of income is dairy. We have set up

women's dairy cooperatives in the fifteen villages where we are working. Now that there are three sources of income, they have a choice whether they should go for farm labour or whether they should stay home and do more work on weaving, spinning or whatever. I must say that, during the last two years, the general rate of minimum wages has gone up in that area.

But the farmers apparently are not yet beaten. Ela Bhatt says they are planning to bring in labourers from outside the area; and she intends to cordon off the area to meet this threat. She is a very courageous woman, but her fifteen villages are just a dot on the vast landscape of India. Changes on the grand scale will only take place when the attitude of the government and its officials alters. Ela Bhatt is very critical of officials.

So often those officials are middle class. They are educated, they are urban, and their whole attitude towards poor people and towards development programmes is that the Government's money is their money, and the poor want to make progress with their money. This is a very cruel statement, but this is the kind of attitude we find all the time.

After years of struggling to improve the lot of casual workers, Ela Bhatt has found some grounds for at least limited optimism. She believes that the poor are now much more aware of the government schemes which are officially available to improve conditions. 'Formerly they didn't have such massive programmes for the eradication of poverty,' she says. 'The government officials at the lower level are now resisting such programmes. Somebody responsible at the highest level should supervise at the local level.'

For a senior officer to supervise at the local level would mean hours and hours of driving around districts in non-airconditioned cars. It would mean patiently listening to disputes in which right is by no means always on the side of the apparently wronged. It would mean clashes with the local political élite, with all the risks of transfer or stay of promotion that would mean. There are very good reasons, therefore, why many senior officials prefer to sit in their offices and learn about the 'successes' of their development programmes from the files.

Farming castes with political influence are one class which benefits from the Neta-Babu Raj; a second is the contractors who control the lives of millions of Indians working in quarries and brick-kilns, on roadworks and building sites, in sweatshops and small factories up and down the land. Many of their labourers are what are known as 'bonded'. This means they are so heavily indebted that they and their families can never leave the contractor's employment. The contractors bribe the officials to get contracts; the officials then turn a blind eye to the workers' pay and conditions.

On the edge of Delhi, there are quarries where workers choke on the dust thrown up by dilapidated stone-crushers. They handle sharp-edged rocks without gloves; they have no goggles to protect their eyes from the chips which fly off their chisels, and no helmets to protect their heads from falling rocks. Their appalling conditions have been the subject of several debates in Parliament only fifteen miles away; but for all the crocodile tears shed by Members of Parliament nothing has changed. Inder Mohan is a social worker who is campaigning for the quarry workers.

> There is no sanitation at all; they all have to defecate in the open somewhere. In the morning, children defecate opposite their huts. The huts are made of some sort of bricks, but not all of them are even made entirely of bricks. Their roofs are hardly roofs. The huts have to be made by the labourers at their own cost. They don't have much money, so they only start building their huts when the contractor advances them money. From that time onwards, they are right under his thumb, because once they borrow money from him there is no hope for them. They cannot run away because the contractor here who brings them from the village knows the money-lender there. He knows the police official there, he knows the politician there, and he knows their counterparts in the city here.

The contractor also does his best to see that his workers

64

become addicted to the illicit liquor all too easily available in the neighbourhood. According to Inder Mohan, this helps the contractor in two ways: 'The liquor benumbs their faculties to react, and they need more money from the contractor to meet their expenses.'

The noise of the lorries and stone-crushers, the heat, the dust, the danger of the quarries are enough to drive anyone to drink. The Government's reaction to pressure from social workers like Inder Mohan, the press and Parliament was to nationalise the quarries. But it could not, or perhaps was not, willing to run them, so they have been handed back to the contractors. It is not the workers who have benefited from nationalisation, but the officials. They now have greater power over the contractors, so they can demand greater rewards. Inder Mohan has no doubt that the problem is once again the Neta-Babu Raj, the political protection that the contractors enjoy.

> There are ministers and leaders in the Congress Party who are hand in glove with the contractors. Some of the ministers and their relatives are even contractors themselves. Of course, they are not registered in their own names. There are certain honest officials within the Delhi Administration, but they are powerless and helpless because the politicians are in this particular racket, politicians not only of Congress but of other parties too. They are playing havoc in this sphere and making a lot of money.

Inder Mohan faces the same problem as Ela Bhatt in trying to organise the quarry workers. There are plenty more where they came from, so troublesome workers can easily be sent home. But Inder Mohan supports Ela Bhatt's view that at least the workers are becoming more aware of their rights. This he believes is a positive achievement.

Some of the worst victims of contractors are children. Mrs Tara Ali Baig is another of the many social workers in India who are struggling for the implementation of the laws to protect labourers. She is the founder of a voluntary scheme which sets up special villages for homeless children. She says it is impossible to prevent child labour, because children are an important economic asset for their families.

We have a very large number of children in the work-force. There are, for instance, estimated to be some seventeen million children who are working in small-scale industries. It's not illegal at all, but it is illegal to employ a child in a hazardous industry. Yet we know from the research we have been doing that there are innumerable children who are working today, with the sanction of the local government, in extremely hazard-ous industries, dealing with sulphur in the match in-dustry, dealing with cyanide – dipping their hands into it – in the brass industry and the glass industry. Government is very alert to this problem, but they say that if we ban child labour it will be a disadvantage to the families themselves.

Mrs Baig particularly remembers one young boy she talked to in Agra.

In Agra everybody comes to see the Taj Mahal, and within a few kilometres of it there is a whole complex of the glass industry which makes electric bulbs, makes glasses for hotels, makes glass for industry, makes the glass bangles women wear. About 50 per cent of the workforce are children. There was this little boy there who told us: 'Yes, I would love to be educated, but there is no time. You see, I have to get up very early and then I work until 9 o'clock at night.'

In India's third economic plan there was a commitment to look upon children as one of the country's richest human resources. Mrs Baig suggested to Jawaharlal Nehru that India should follow the pattern laid down in countries like Israel where enormous investments had been made in every stage of a child's development. Nehru's reply was: 'Well, it's much more complex in India, and we have to wait for evolution.' Mrs Baig believes that, in spite of all the problems that still remain to be solved, there has been evolution. 'Children are much better looked after today,' she says, 'and there's much more opportu-nity also. There is educational opportunity and income-gener-ating opportunity too. Mothers are much more enlightened in a way. The problem is the degree to which they can make their husbands and their mothers-in-law follow them.'

In spite of the evolution which has undoubtedly taken place, the barbaric practice of forcing children to beg does still survive. 'There are beggar-lords,' says Mrs Baig, 'who have armies of little children working for them. Some of them are mutilated. These children have been kidnapped. The child is then taken to some other place where it is quite helpless, so it does what it is told to do.' Nevertheless, Mrs Baig says that begging is not a 'major factor' in the overall problem. Most of the children working in the bigger cities of India have migrated with their parents. Urban migration is causing apparently insuperable problems for cities like Bombay, Calcutta and now Delhi too. Corruption and political interference prevent the implementation of the planning regulations. Officials turn a blind eye to the illegal occupation of land, because the slum-dwellers promise their votes to the politicians in return for protection from the law.

Congress Party flags were fluttering from the roofs of the Jayaprakash Nagar slum in Bhopal the night of the famous gas disaster. The next morning in the narrow alleys and sordid shacks only the dead remained, deserted by those who, blinded and choked by the gas, had managed to drag themselves away from the disaster. The slum was just across the road from the Union Carbide plant, in defiance of every safety regulation. The Congress flags showed that the ruling party had sanctioned this, sentencing the slum-dwellers to be the victims of the worst man-made disaster in history.

Of course, there are economic as well as political reasons for the slums. The problem can't be solved simply by implementing the planning laws. Bombay, India's commercial capital, is bursting at the seams. The heart of the city still retains its Victorian–Saracenic–Gothic splendour. The elaborately ornate Victoria Terminus makes even St Pancras look plain. But for the most part, Bombay is now a city of skyscrapers and slums. Many of the slum-dwellers are single men who have come to the city in search of work and left their wives and children in their villages. They are often supporting parents, brothers and sisters too.

In the Bombay slum of Jawaharnagar, named after Nehru to please the Congress Party, the rows of shacks with their tin roofs are divided by narrow alleys just four feet wide, with open drains down the middle of them. The living conditions seem grim enough to defeat the most resilient spirits, but they do not defeat the Bombay slum-dweller. The shacks are clean and decorated inside. Many of the children are smartly dressed and sent to school regularly. There is a temple on the corner of one of the alleys, and a flourishing bazaar on the edge of the slum. Life certainly goes on in Jawaharnagar. Mrs Vipula Kadri is a social worker who has founded an organisation which is attempting to stem the flood of humanity into Bombay, in fact to reverse it and persuade slum-dwellers to go back to their villages.

> I feel there are great chances of people from the slums going back to their own villages. They do want to go back. We have already taken back about thirty-two boys who were from the slums. I don't think they ever talk about Bombay or the movies or the slums. Everybody thinks that all these people come to Bombay because of the glamour that it offers. I think it's more than that. It's work, it's money.

Mrs Kadri believes that the answer to the slums of the cities is to provide more work in the countryside. The right-wing Hindu Shiv Sena, a political party which wants Bombay to be the preserve of the people of its own state, Maharashtra, is campaigning to drive the slum-dwellers out of the city. Their view is an extreme view; but there are many politicians in more moderate parties who would at least like to see the pavement-dwellers cleared away.

A typical pavement-dweller is Mr Krishnaswamy, who lives in a tent made out of black plastic sheeting on a busy pavement just outside the docks. He has lived there for thirty-five years. Ten times now the police have cleared him and his family off the pavement, taken them into what he calls the jungle, and dropped them there. Ten times Mr Krishnaswamy has come back to his pavement. 'The municipality,' he explains, 'does not want us to be here, but where else can we go. They don't give us anywhere else to live.' Mr Krishnaswamy is no down-and-out. He is a registered dock-worker. Like any good father, he has ambitions for his family. He wants his son to learn English, because he thinks that will help him to get on. In spite of his appalling living conditions, Mr Krishnaswamy lives a comparatively full life.

Shrilatha Batliwala is a member of a voluntary organisation, SPARC, which is fighting a battle against those like the Shiv Sena who want to sweep Mr Krishnaswamy off the streets. She does not believe that it is possible to persuade urban migrants to go back to their villages.

We all tend to say that urbanisation is a terrible thing, and city life is so awful. It has been our experience that many people have found city life preferable to their rural existence. For example, the caste rigidity completely breaks down in an urban area. People who became landless and belonged to high castes in their villages found they could not survive in the village, because they were not permitted by their caste-fellows to take up manual labour or other occupations to earn an income. They were, in fact, forced to migrate and leave the village, so that they wouldn't put this stigma on the rest of their caste. They came to Bombay as long ago as twenty years and have lived here and done fairly well for themselves and now have the means, if they so wish, to buy land and go back to their village; but none of them want to. Here they feel they're free to live as they want, to do as they want, and to follow any occupation, without any stigma being attached to it. But they can in no way afford any kind of proper housing in the city. The housing market is astronomically expensive. Slum huts cost anything between 10 000 and 25 000 rupees [£5000 to £12 000]. No labourer can save that in an entire lifetime, so the only feasible alternative for them is to settle on the pavement.

The Bombay Municipality has tried resettling some of the pavement-dwellers in special housing and subsidising their transport to work, but Mrs Batliwala does not think that is the answer.

I really wonder whether the conditions in the so-called transit camps and colonies where people have been moved in the past are all that much better than on a pavement. This kind of solution does not take into consideration the fact that their occupations are intimately linked to their living in a certain place. Transport is extremely expensive. People pursuing certain kinds of occupation like handcart pullers will not be able to take the handcart on a bus or train. Some kind of alternative which is based on a study of the occupational needs of these people is necessary.

Even living on the pavements is not all that cheap in Bombay, as Mrs Batliwala explains.

Pavements have been captured by certain strong men, many of whom don't live themselves on the pavement but in neighbouring tenements. People have paid either for outright purchase of a 6 foot by 6 foot stretch of pavement up to 5000 rupees to my knowledge, or they are paying rent to the tune of 50 rupees per month. Another interesting example of how these musclemen operate is capturing public toilets. Most pavement-dwellers who have a public toilet prefer to use that to open defecation, naturally. Now, what these chaps do is to get control of certain toilets and charge people half a rupee each time they go to the toilet. When we were talking to women about some of their health problems, a lot of them complained of urinary infections and other related diseases. They said: 'We know why we have these problems. It's because we only go twice a day, and once a day if we can help it, early morning and late at night, because if we have to go more often than that, it means spending more than one or two rupees a day just to use the toilet.'

So spending a penny can be an expensive business in Bombay, since a rupee is worth five pence, which in slum-dwellers' terms is a substantial part of the day's earnings.

Landless labourers in Bihar, children working in sweat-shops, the pavement-dwellers of Bombay, these are the unacceptable face of Indian industrialisation. It is a face which Indians themselves recognise as unacceptable. It is criticised in the press almost daily, debated in Parliament and the state assemblies. Voluntary workers up and down the land crusade against it. But there is another face to India. It can be seen in the government programme for feeding schoolchildren in the southern state of Tamil Nadu, in the land reforms pushed through in the teeth of opposition from large farmers in Marxist West Bengal, and in the rural prosperity of green-belt states like Haryana.

The Raipur Rani block is in Haryana. A block is the smallest administrative unit. Each one has its own development officer, who in true bureaucratic fashion can all too easily become 'the officer who blocks development'. In Raipur Rani that is certainly not the case. In one of the villages, there is now a High School attended by almost as many girls as boys. The headmistress says that the dropout rate up to the age of sixteen is only one per cent. She puts this down to special efforts the Haryana Government has made to get parents to send their children to school. The village now has a tarmac road and a regular bus service. There is electricity, but the villagers have also taken to alternative sources of energy. There are two large plants for producing gas from cow-dung. They did also try a windmill but did not find it much use. In many houses, the old stoves which used to pour smoke into the eyes and lungs of housewives have been replaced by new smokeless and fuel-efficient ones. The chairman of the village *panchayat* or committee, Prem Chand, is in no doubt about the reason for all this progress.

> Previously we only got a very low yield from our land; now the crop has increased. There were water problems; now we have tubewells. The government has paid attention to the problems of water, electricity and fertilisers, and now we have tractors.

So the Neta-Babu Raj has had its successes too.

OLD GODS FOR NEW

Hinduism is the backbone, the heart and the soul of Indian civilisation. It is entirely Indian, never having sought to extend its sway by proselytising. Its garish gods, its outlandish legends, its lack of authoritative scriptures, of Church and canon law, make Hinduism almost impossible to comprehend for those brought up in the comparative certainties of religions of the Book; but some effort must be made to understand Hinduism if we are to get anywhere near to understanding India itself.

Tirupati, in the southern state of Andhra Pradesh, is reputed to be the richest Hindu temple in India. We drove there in a battered Hindustan Ambassador, an Indian version of the Morris Oxford of the fifties which is still manufactured near Calcutta. It barely made it up the hills known as the Eastern Ghats, in which the huge complex surrounding the Tirupati temple is set.

We were accompanied by a remarkable couple – the Ramamurthys. Although we had never met them before, they had, with typical Indian hospitality, agreed to be our guides to the mysteries of Tirupati. Mr Ramamurthy, with his shock of greying, curly, unkempt hair, his rounded shoulders and his stoop, looks like a scholar. He did indeed win a Rhodes Scholarship to Oxford and has a deep knowledge of Hinduism. By profession, however, Mr Ramamurthy is a civil servant, a member of the Indian Administrative Service or IAS, the élite cadre which replaced the British Indian Civil Service or ICS. Because of his high standing in the IAS, Mr Ramamurthy was able to arrange for us to receive VIP treatment at Tirupati.

We entered the temple through a modern concrete building like an airport lounge which has been constructed to control the thousands of pilgrims who flock to Tirupati. The new arrangements are functional and the buildings spotlessly clean, but they make no attempt to blend with the ancient temple. The present temple was first built in the fourteenth century. Like the cathedrals of Europe, parts have been destroyed and parts have been added down the centuries. Like many cathedrals, too, the twentieth-century additions have been the least successful architecturally.

When we entered the dark halls of the temple proper, the wedding of the temple deity, Lord Venkateshwara, to Lakshmi, the goddess of wealth, and Bhoo Devi, the Earth Mother, was being celebrated by Brahmin priests. They were chanting the *Vedas* to the accompaniment of accordions, drums, and a bassoon-like instrument known as the *nadaswaram*. When the wedding ended, the three small images of the deities were taken back to their resting places, this time to the raucous sound of conch-shells. As the procession passed, the Ramamurthys and other members of the congregation prostrated themselves before the deities.

Tirupati is a centre of pilgrimage for both Shaivites and Vaishnavites, the two great schools of Hinduism. This is one reason why it is such an important place of pilgrimage. The other is that Lord Venkateshwara himself has a great reputation as an effective god, one who answers prayers and grants boons. There is no need for a notice appealing to visitors to contribute generously to Tirupati's upkeep. The money literally pours into the *hundi*, the cavernous, canvas bag in which the faithful drop their offerings. Grateful devotees make many other offerings too. Some shave their heads; some give silver images of the part of their body which has been healed by Lord Venkateshwara; some even slip guns into the *hundi* – presumably in gratitude for a mission accomplished or as a guarantee of real repentance.

The priests we saw celebrating the wedding of Lord Venkateshwara, or reciting his hundred names for individual worshippers, come from families who have served the temple for centuries. In the neighbouring state of Tamil Nadu, democracy has now entered the temples. There temple priesthoods are open, officially at least, to anyone who has the theological qualifications. Tirupati, too, has not shut itself off entirely from the twentieth century. It now has a modern university, and the priests are broadening their studies. Mr Ramamurthy introduced us to Dr Ramana Dikshitulu, the head-priest. At thirty-six, he is young for a holder of that office. His hair flows loose over his shoulders; his forelock has been shaved; he is bare-chested, with the sacred thread of a Hindu Brahmin over one shoulder, and wears a white loin-cloth. Dr Dikshitulu's family have been priests at Tirupati for six hundred years, and he too looks every inch the traditional priest; but his doctorate was in microbiology not theology. He symbolises India, a land where the ancient is not preserved in aspic, but is alive and mingling with the modern.

Dr Dikshitulu invited us into the *sanctum sanctorum*, a dark, pillared chamber, lit only by flickering oil-lamps. The oil was *ghee* or liquefied butter. Lord Venkateshwara's statue stood some eight feet tall against the far wall, garlanded from head to toe with flowers, precious stones and gold. His eyes were covered with camphor, because the faithful are afraid of his gaze. The *darshan*, or sight of the Lord, is the supreme moment of a pilgrimage, and we found it deeply moving. As we left the chamber, priests offered us holy water and placed inverted silver chalices on our heads as a symbol of submission to the Lord.

Because of the Old Testament strictures against idolatry, temple worship seems little short of blasphemy to Christians, Muslims and Jews. Many Hindus also regard it as superstition; but temple worship has a deep meaning to Mr Ramamurthy.

I don't think it is superstition or empty, because you cannot expect all devotees to have the same level of aspiration or achievement in seeking closeness with the Lord. There would be people who can concentrate on a flame, or even the image of a flame which is in their minds, and see the Almighty in it. But for the vast majority of people, they'd like to see something concrete, as a cross might be for the Christian, so that you can see the Lord and feel that you have been in communion with the Lord.

Ramamurthy points out that there is unity in the amazing diversity of the Hindu pantheon. He explains that Hinduism is in fact a monotheistic religion: 'Hindus believe that there is one God. In fact they go beyond Christians because they also believe that we are all part of that one God. All the idols, as you call them, are just manifestations of that one God.'

Hinduism has survived the sword of Islam and Christian persecution. According to Badrinath Chaturvedi, the author of a major work on Indian civilisation, its great strength is its ideological flexibility.

> One of the principles of Indian thought has been that all ideas are only an approximation to the truth. Therefore, no idea represents the whole truth. As a consequence, Indians developed an attitude towards other opinions and ideas which was very accepting. Everything was valid; so that the question was not between truth and untruth, or what was right and wrong, but between incomplete perceptions and, relatively speaking, more complete perceptions. This accounts, I think, for the Indian tolerance, hospitality, understanding of other people's problems. They do not take a very rigid stand on ideas. You and I may violently disagree on a certain point and yet continue to be friends.

Because of this unique tolerance Islam and Christianity still flourish in India, though both have been deeply influenced by Hinduism. Nowhere is this more obvious than in the case of caste and Christianity. The Church teaches that all people are equal. Yet there are Roman Catholic dioceses in India where it has only recently been possible to persuade high-caste Christians to accept *Harijan* or Untouchable priests. The high-caste Christians couldn't quite rid themselves of the fear that they would be polluted if they took communion from the hands of an Untouchable.

Old religions tend to be conservative, and Hinduism is no exception. The forty years of Indian independence can be seen as a battle between the tenacious conservatism of the Hindu ethos and the modern forces unleashed by Nehru's revolution. Nowhere is this more apparent than in the battle against caste, the traditional hierarchy into which Hindus divided society according to the jobs people did. It is one of the many paradoxes of modern India that although discrimination by caste has been outlawed, most politicians admit that caste, not ideology, continues to dominate Indian politics. George Fernandes, the Socialist politician, believes that it is caste which has prevented the growth of national parties based on ideologies.

> The caste system in India has been exploited; it has been exploited by the opposition as well as the ruling party. Everybody tries to capitalise on it for limited electoral advantage without realising that, in the long term, this becomes the main thrust of their political activity. That's what it has become today. Therefore, whatever efforts we make to bring ideological coherence into our politics are still running into difficulties. When we campaign, people are interested in socialist answers; but when it comes to the vote, they would like to vote for the man who belongs to their caste. So if in every constituency you can produce the man who belongs to the caste which can clinch the vote, then your socialism through that candidate is o.k. But if it's socialism with a party that does not accept this old caste divide, then it's not acceptable.

But George Fernandes is not disheartened. 'It is still possible to have a political revolution, change through political means,' he says. 'I don't think we will have to wait very long for it. I will be around, and I will see it happen in this country.'

Important changes have already taken place in the caste system, and they have affected politics. Since independence, *Harijans* have been guaranteed certain seats in state assemblies and Parliament and a percentage of government jobs and educational opportunities. These reserved opportunities, or 'reservations' as they are known, have produced a new *Harijan* leadership, and a new party has been formed to represent their interests, the *Bahujan Samaj*. Its leader is Kanshi Ram, a

Harijan who benefited from reservations and became a government employee. Seeing how few *Harijans* were able to benefit from reservations, he decided it was necessary to launch a direct attack on what he saw as the entrenched position of the upper castes. Kanshi Ram believes that the upper castes 'openly condemn caste but secretly preserve it.' One of their most potent weapons, according to him, is the cult of Mahatma Gandhi as the saviour of the *Harijans*.

> Education has been so arranged by the ruling groups that they select such heroes as Gandhi. What has Gandhi done? He fought tooth and nail against the interests of the downtrodden people. In September 1932, he went on fast against reservations. Later it was propagated that Gandhi was responsible for reservations. He was a great hypocrite, to my mind. He lived in a sweepers' [*Harijan*] colony and he told them: 'Your job is a very good job, you are doing a very good job. If I am to be born again I would like to be born as a sweeper.' He was told: 'If you want to be a sweeper, we can fulfil your desire in this life. Come on.' But he never came. He was a hypocrite just fooling innocent people.

Kanshi Ram believes that reserving some seats in assemblies and Parliament for *Harijans* has just produced political *chamchas* or stooges. It has, in his view, 'played into the hands of the higher castes.' But he does accept that the reservation of jobs has helped.

> In the administration and in the government services, since 1963 the quota has always been full. So now the *Harijans* and the tribals have 22 per cent of the government jobs. They are next only to the Brahmins. Whatever we have acquired, we have acquired because of these job reservations. It has very much helped us in building this movement.

Kanshi Ram feels that the position of *Harijans* has changed so much since independence that a separate electorate would no longer be in their interests. His movement is trying to unite the *Harijans* with other castes he believes are still oppressed by those at the top of the caste-tree. That, he maintains, will form an electorate of between 80 and 85 per cent of the voters. His movement is now having some impact on elections in Uttar Pradesh, India's most populous state.

Mahatma Gandhi undoubtedly did awake India to the scandal of untouchability; but it can be argued that his insistence that Untouchables should not organise themselves into a separate party, and should seek their salvation within the Congress, prevented the growth of a national *Harijan* movement.

Arun Shourie, a prominent journalist and author of a book on Hinduism, sees something of a paradox in the fact that caste's influence on day-to-day life is declining, but not its influence on politics.

> There is a multiplicity of castes now that are operating. There's more jostling, and therefore a greater option for the electorate than was the case say in the late forties and the early fifties. But with new opportunities coming up, either for political office or for the funds of the state, everybody retreats to the group he knows, either caste or region or religion, so as to be able to organise himself around something to get at that fruit. But my overall view is that in life in general caste is much less important than it is in politics. Fifty years ago, if an Untouchable's shadow fell on a south Indian Brahmin, he would go and bathe six times. Now in an overcrowded bus does anyone verify who is the person who is crushing him? So many people also go to restaurants now. Everybody takes water from the municipal tap. Do people verify which is the hand on the other side of the tap? So I think technology is corroding caste in our lives, but new opportunities are reinforcing caste in our relations with the state. Ultimately it is technology which will prevail.

In spite of Nehru's efforts to establish India as a secular democracy, religion is re-emerging as a major factor in Indian politics. Hindus are beginning to feel that secularism means their interests are sacrificed to keep the minorities, particularly the Muslims, happy. This view is articulated by the right-wing,

Hindu Bhartiya Janata Party. Its most popular orator is Atal Behari Vajpayee, who was India's Foreign Minister during the late seventies.

We do feel that Hindus should not be discriminated against in this country simply because they are in the majority. If the minorities are pampered, if there is no common civil code of law just because orthodox Muslims are opposed to it, then it creates an impression in the Hindu mind that things are not moving in the right direction. Just because political parties are more interested in getting votes from the minorities than in building a really non-communal structure. I'll give you a concrete example. There was a Hindu Professor in Delhi University who wanted to re-marry. As a Hindu he could not; but he had decided to get rid of his wife; so he embraced Islam and then he re-married. The laws relating to marriage, divorce, inheritance, should be the same for everyone.

Some Muslim leaders, however, say they fear that they will soon find themselves living in a Hindu state. Vajpayee dismisses these fears: 'They are baseless. Hindus by nature are tolerant. Their outlook is catholic. We want equal treatment for all but no special privileges for any community.'

Nevertheless even Vajpayee admits that the communal riots which flare up every year show that Hinduism's traditional tolerance is breaking down.

It is true that now Hindus have started to retaliate in a very strong manner, and that should be a matter of concern to all political parties, particularly those who talk of secularism. Hindus are becoming communal and I'm not happy at this state of affairs. I am worried about the future.

Muslims are becoming more militant too. The Jama Masjid, one of Asia's largest mosques, dominates the old city of Delhi. The crowded narrow alleys, the colourful shops, the food stalls, are in sharp contrast to the drab uniformity of modern Delhi. The mosque was built by the Moghul emperor Shah

Jahan, the builder of the Taj Mahal, and the old city still retains much of the atmosphere of Moghul times. The Imam or head clergyman of the Jama Masjid is still called the *Shahi* or Royal Imam. A vast man, who wears flowing robes and a skull-cap stuck on the back of his shaved head, he is very much a political prelate. During the 1977 election, he campaigned vigorously for the Janata Party. In the next election, Mrs Gandhi anxiously solicited his help to bring her back to power. The Imam did eventually strike a bargain with Mrs Gandhi, but she did not fulfil it to his satisfaction. He again became a bitter opponent of the Congress Party, using his pulpit to preach the need for Muslims to fight for their rights. His son, the Deputy Imam, has formed a militant organisation known as the Army of Adam, to do the fighting.

At partition, the Muslim League leaders went to Pakistan, handing the field over to the Congress Muslims. Because of dissatisfaction with the recent record of the Congress Party, efforts are now being made to establish a new and independent Muslim leadership. The Imam certainly regards himself as one candidate, but his influence is limited and his politics are extreme. Syed Shahabuddin, diplomat turned politician, is a more widely accepted spokesman for the Muslim community. He blames Mrs Gandhi for much of the tension between the two communities, accusing her of deserting the secularism which was the cornerstone of her father's policy.

It's not that Mrs Gandhi suddenly turned communal; but I do feel that for political reasons she adopted communal tactics. I think she deliberately made a change in 1980, because she felt that the Muslim vote had shifted away from her. She decided she had to devise a new combination as her electoral base, and therefore she tried to establish a Hindu sense of identity. She showed a Hindu face.

Shahabuddin believes it was the Emergency,[1] imposed in 1975, which marked the break between Mrs Gandhi and the Muslims of India.

Some of the happenings of the Emergency were re-

1   See Chapter 8.

sented by the Muslim community. I believe for example that they bore the brunt of the family planning programme. There was forcible sterilisation in some places. Then again, there were the slum-clearance schemes. The schemes may have been motivated by good motives, but it is the Muslim community which mainly lives in the slums of the big towns, and so they bore the brunt of the demolitions. All this contributed to the alienation of the Muslim community during the Emergency; and so when the elections of 1977 came, broadly speaking the Muslim vote switched away from the Congress.

Shahabuddin believes that the Muslims do have very real grievances.

I do find a pattern of discrimination against Muslim villages, Muslim localities in towns, Muslim pockets of population, and this is what I resent. The government ought to treat all people alike. Why is it that the Muslim localities in any town are the least cared for by the local municipality? Why is it that primary schools are not being established on the basis of the official ratio of schools to population in Muslim villages? This is the pattern of discrimination that we are against. Because of this discrimination, I am conscious of a growing sense of restiveness among Muslim youth. They feel that they are victims of inequality – that they don't get jobs, they don't get education. All this builds up, and they say: 'We have got to start a struggle.' It would certainly be a very unfortunate day for our country if things came to such a pass that the Hindus and Muslims were at each other's throats throughout the length and breadth of India. It will not remain a localised problem.

Shahabuddin believes that there can still be a political solution which will satisfy the aspirations of the Muslim community, but he does not believe that the answer lies in forming a special Muslim party. That has been tried, he points out.

I personally maintain that the Muslim community

82

cannot resolve its problems in isolation from the main political stream of the country. The Muslim faces the same problems as any other citizen does, and so he has to participate in the common struggle. On Muslim questions, on matters of special importance to the Muslim community, we must have a framework, a platform, to help formulate Muslim public opinion. It should not participate directly as a party in politics. We do have an organisation of this sort, the Muslim *Mushawarat*. We who are involved in the various Muslim movements get together under its umbrella. We meet each other, and we talk to each other across party lines. We do whatever we can in our personal capacities and within the political system or party to which we belong.

There are, of course, many Muslims who still believe that the best answer for their community is to return to their old allegiance to the Congress Party. In fact, M. J. Akbar, the editor of the Calcutta daily *The Telegraph* and the author of a book on the problems of India's minorities, says that the Muslims have not really deserted Congress.

I would certainly not agree with those who say that the Muslims have lost their faith in the Congress Party. Mrs Gandhi certainly did make good use of the politics which aimed at creating a Hindu majority sentiment. But then look at the general election held just after she died. The Muslims all voted for Rajiv Gandhi. The paradox lies in the simple fact that whatever the Congress Party may be at any given moment – whether it is more or less pro-Muslim – no other party has been able to win the confidence of the minorities.

M. J. Akbar does not believe that there is any danger of the Muslims of India supporting Islamic fundamentalism, or fundamentalist parties.

That is just not going to happen. If it was, it should have happened when the situation was far worse for the Muslims. Take the communal riots in 1964 in

Bengal, which were, I think, the worst phase of communalism in Bengal. It was a bad time for the rest of the country too. It seemed as though the secular fabric of India was in tatters, and the country was on fire. There was also a famine in the land and a growing feeling of despair. People felt that after twenty years the Congress had not been able to deliver, to provide food, to protect lives. That was why the Congress was routed in elections. But even then, the alternatives the minorities sought or looked for were not the communal parties. In Bengal, for instance, the alternative they found was the Left.

India has only one Muslim-majority state, Kashmir, and there Islamic fundamentalism does pose a political threat, as we found when we visited the state during elections to its Assembly in 1987. Fundamentalist parties, some of which openly support Pakistan in its dispute with India over the status of Kashmir, had formed an alliance to fight the elections. The state is still divided between India and Pakistan although the beautiful Kashmir valley remains entirely in India.

During the summer, the valley of Kashmir is one place which really does live up to the holiday brochures. It is a paradise, with its emerald-green rice-fields, saffron, fragrant fruit-blossoms, and almost every flower known to man. Alpine meadows, pine-forests, and magnificent lakes are surrounded by the mighty Himalayas. Its fast-running streams are full of trout. Yet, when we arrived, Kashmir was anything but paradise. The spring was late, so the trees were still bare, and the melted snow had left the valley a dirty brown. There was not a flower to be seen. It had been a harsh winter, and everyone was still talking of the hardships caused by shortages of fuel and power.

The grim winter had not dampened the Kashmiris' enthusiasm for elections. We drove into the countryside with Begum Abdullah, the widow of the legendary Sheikh Abdullah, the 'Lion of Kashmir', whose family has dominated the politics of the state since independence. Every time her car stopped, her supporters gathered to pay their homage to the woman they call 'Benevolent Mother'. In one village where she was scheduled to address a meeting, the Begum's car was stopped by a procession. As she stepped out, a sea of shoving and shouting supporters closed over her and, miraculously without hurting the old lady, carried her along to the platform from which she was to address the meeting. But for all their enthusiasm, the villagers were worried about the latest developments in Kashmiri politics.

The Nehrus have never quite known what to do with the Abdullahs. They have always needed them as a bulwark against Pakistani attempts to win the loyalty of Kashmiris; but at the same time they have been reluctant to see the Abdullahs become all-powerful. Nehru imprisoned Sheikh Abdullah, the founder of the dynasty, and Mrs Gandhi signed an agreement with him that brought him back to power. When the old man died, Rajiv Gandhi rashly fought with his son, Dr Farooq Abdullah. Eventually Rajiv Gandhi had to eat humble pie and form an alliance with Dr Abdullah. The Prime Minister recognised the Abdullahs' suzerainty over Kashmir, in return for his own Congress Party being allowed to retain a foothold in the Valley. Many of the followers of the Abdullahs resented this alliance; they could not understand why the family they supported so loyally should need the help of anyone else to win elections in Kashmir. Begum Abdullah admits that it has not been easy to explain this to her followers.

> Sometimes Sheikh Sahib's followers have asked me why we had to form this alliance with Rajiv Gandhi's Congress Party. I have had to explain to them that this is a bridge. I have come close to the Congress Party because without the co-operation of the central government there is no way ahead for us.

The Begum maintains that there has never been any doubt about her family's loyalty to India; but she does not feel that loyalty has been repaid.

> It gives me joy to see that our people give my family such love and respect. We have not been able to give them anything in return, because we are not free, and that is why we feel choked. We have been one of the most gentle states, in the sense that we have always tried to keep our people calm and not to behave in a way that will create law and order problems.

India will have to handle its relations with the Abdullahs very carefully if Kashmir is to remain a gentle state. The Muslims, of course, are not the only restless community in India. Until the 1980s, communal tension between Hindus and Sikhs was almost unthinkable. The Sikhs had their demands and pursued them vigorously; but they also emerged as one of the most prosperous communities, spread throughout India and well integrated wherever they lived. Yet, in 1984, Delhi was to be the scene of anti-Sikh riots which were more violent than anything India had seen since the massacres of partition; and they were to be sparked off by the assassination of Prime Minister Indira Gandhi by two Sikh members of her bodyguard.[1]

When Mrs Gandhi died, the secularism her father had bequeathed India seemed to be in tatters. Many Muslims were divorced from the Congress Party, which had once been the vehicle for Nehru's secular politics. The Sikhs were hurt and angry; and for the first time, a significant section of that progressive community wondered whether they really did have a place in the Indian Union. The Hinduism which had created modern India's unity in diversity with its unique tolerance of other religions, was now being ruthlessly exploited as a political weapon against the minorities.

[1] See Chapter 9.

GODDESSES REBORN

A major paradox of Indian society over the centuries has been its ambivalent attitude to women. The segregation and veiling of Indian women has been a relatively recent development which accompanied the Muslim invasions and settlement of the north from the twelfth century onwards. It was introduced partly to protect Hindu women from the attentions of Muslim conquerers, and partly in imitation of the harems of Muslim rulers. But while Hindu women have traditionally had more personal freedom than their Muslim counterparts, they have suffered serious discrimination in matrimonial and family law since the earliest period of Aryan settlement of the sub-continent. Male supremacy was enshrined in the *Vedas*, the ancient Hindu scriptures; but it was superimposed upon pre-Aryan civilisations, dating back to 5000 BC, which had a strongly matriarchal bias and celebrated the cult of the Mother-Goddess. The result was a peculiarly Indian compromise, in which women could be both goddesses and slaves, matriarchs and chattels.

Indian nationalists recognised early on that the emancipation of women would be a crucial factor in their struggle for independence. Not only was the female half of the population a necessary support for mass movements, but the status of women would be a key indicator of India's capacity to modernise itself and overcome the stigma of backwardness. The colonial rulers, in alliance with enlightened Hindu reformers like Raja Ram Mohan Roy,[1] had initiated this process in the

1 The pioneer of the Bengali renaissance, Roy founded the Brahmo Samaj movement, which drew on Western education and Christian ethics to create a reformed Hinduism.

mid-nineteenth century with legislation to abolish *sati*[1] and female infanticide and to permit the re-marriage of widows. The Hindu cultural renaissance of the late nineteenth century emphasised that, if Hinduism were to survive, it must cleanse itself of caste prejudice and the oppression of women.

By the 1920s, Mahatma Gandhi had carried this conviction into the political arena with his appeal to women to abandon their traditional seclusion and join the ranks of his *satyagrahis*.[2] When the Congress Party in 1930 adopted full independence as its goal, it also committed itself to equality for women. In the civil disobedience campaigns that followed, thousands of women, educated and illiterate, affluent and working-class, put aside their domestic preoccupations to march in Congress demonstrations, face police batons and court imprisonment. There are Indian women activists today who feel that the optimism of those nationalist years has not been fulfilled by independence. Among them is Ela Bhatt, a tireless voluntary worker on behalf of poorer working women, and now a member of the Indian Parliament.

> Gandhi had perceived women as forerunners of the social transformation in nation-building. He had more faith in women, that they would be able to do this better than men, and this was accepted in the Congress. But after we got independence, somehow this did not happen; maybe because at that time it was mainly educated, middle-class women who were leaders of the women's movement. When we got freedom, women like me, who had got the benefits of the new system, forgot about poor women.

For the vast majority of Indian women, the problem is not one of legal equality, but of achieving the educational skills, self-confidence and economic muscle to implement the equal rights enshrined in India's statute books. Their major legal disabilities were swept away by enlightened legislation in the decade after independence; and here, as in other spheres, it was the country's first prime minister, Jawaharlal Nehru, who led the way. His sweeping reform of Hindu family law was opposed,

1 The practice of self-immolation by Hindu windows.
2 Passive resisters.

not only by right-wing fundamentalists, but by orthodox Hindus in Congress, including India's first president, Dr Rajendra Prasad. The Prime Minister ignored the President's opposition and pushed through the new Hindu Code, as it was called. It was a major milestone in the march towards equality, giving women an equal share of family property and protecting their rights in marriage and divorce. Of course, altering the law does not by itself alter social attitudes and practice. But according to Tara Ali Baig, one of India's most prominent social workers, the spread of female education has led to important changes.

> Families themselves never thought it was necessary to educate girls, because they said the girl has to go to another family and must therefore learn everything at home about how to care for others, so that she is an honour to her family when she gets married. They thought that household care, helping the mother and looking after the baby sister or brother, was much more important than education. But that has changed dramatically; and one of the indicators of this is a phenomenon you get in the dailies – especially the English dailies in big cities like Delhi, Calcutta and Bombay – the matrimonial page. In the old days, the matrimonial page used to say that they wanted a girl who was skilled in Household Arts; there were nice, little abbreviations, H. A. and that sort of thing. Now, if you go systematically down these pages, in almost all of them it's a question of wanting a highly educated girl. That is an indicator, if there ever was, of the change that has taken place.

Despite this change of expectations, parents anxious to arrange marriages for their children still scan the classified advertisements every Sunday. 'Match wanted for highly educated Punjabi *Khatri*[1] girl,' says a typical, recent advertisement. It goes on to describe her physical attributes – '159 centimetres high, pretty and fair-skinned' – and ends by assuring potential husbands that she comes from 'a respectable family'. Such advertisements certainly indicate that women

1 An upper caste.

are still widely regarded as goods and chattels, a view reinforced by the fact that dowry, although illegal, is still regularly demanded by the bridegroom's family.

There are many thoughtful Indians, some of them far from reactionary, who defend the basic principle of arranged marriages. One of them is Dr Anandalakshmy, principal of the Lady Irwin College for women in Delhi. When she asks the girls in her classes whether they would like to select their own partners, the majority, she says, still prefer their families to make the choice.

> They say that their parents would know how to make the right choice, because they would choose from the right kind of group. It's partly related to the fact that we do not have any real, institutional arrangements for young people to meet together, so there is no situation really where they can meet people casually, without any intention of marriage. If you meet a person only with the intention of marriage, you have to say either yes or no immediately; and that's very tough. So they feel the arranged marriage system gives them a bit of flexibility. What they always say is: 'We have the veto. We don't have to accept, and we can always say no.'

The headman of a village in the northern state of Haryana puts the advantages of an arranged marriage more earthily. 'In England,' he says, 'you fall in love before marriage and out after it. In India, we fall in love after marriage and stay in love.' Arranged marriages, purged of the element of coercion which applied to women, and sometimes to men too, may well have their advantages.

But although attitudes to women are changing, there is evidence that the old prejudice against girls has far from disappeared. Tara Ali Baig says that it is actually being reinforced, sometimes in frightening ways, by modern technology.

> There was a saying in the ancient *Upanishads*[1]: 'Lord, here grant a boy; grant a girl elsewhere'. If a boy was born, there was tremendous celebration, and sweets

1   Sanskrit religious commentaries on the *Vedas*.

were distributed. But if a girl was born, there was lamentation in the house, and everyone would come and tell the poor woman: 'Perhaps next time you'll have a boy'. That still persists; the concept of a boy being more important than a girl has not vanished. A very modern change that's taken place, and one that's been very alarming to all of us in the welfare field, is that, with the development of amniocentesis, there are doctors in certain small towns who are advertising that they can determine the sex of an unborn child. And those families then have abortions; so it's a modern version of female infanticide that's taking place.

As Indian women's organisations point out, the new is by no means always better than the old. In India's overcrowded industrial cities, the traditional respect for women is breaking down, and violence against them is on the increase. *Saheli*, a collective of radical feminists in Delhi, blames the *goonda* or gangster mentality of the growing numbers of unemployed youth in the cities. Kalpana Mehta, a member of *Saheli*, points out that in cases of rape, the delays and insensitivity shown by the police and the courts offer women little redress from the criminal law.

When women have just been raped, they are very full of anger, and they are willing to fight back and see to it that people are punished. What is very important here is the kind of delay which takes place – three, four, five years – after the rape has occurred. What happens then is that the woman has forgotten the anger at one level, and secondly has moved on in life. She might have got married and is very afraid that now, when the case comes up, what will happen if she gives witness? The third thing is that the rapists are often let out on bail, and then they go and terrorise the families concerned. When the case comes up four or five years later, we face this kind of problem where the woman comes and says: 'Please can you do something to help me, so that I don't have to give evidence now.'

An even more sinister form of violence against women is

dowry-death, when a husband or his family burns a newly married woman because she has not brought enough money with her. The murders are often disguised as kitchen accidents; and here again, says Kalpana Mehta of *Saheli*, the police are invariably slow, and often reluctant, to investigate.

A more everyday hazard faced by urban women is the form of harassment quaintly described by the Indian police as 'eve-teasing'. The term covers a wide range of physical and verbal molestation of women in public places, including the ubiquitous bottom-pinching that goes on in overcrowded Delhi buses. 'It's one of those strange cities,' says Kalpana Mehta, 'where every time a woman boards a bus, she is prepared to be pinched, to be touched unnecessarily, to have people fall all over her. And she has to be prepared to retaliate or to bear it in silence.' According to Principal Ananda-lakshmy of Lady Irwin College, many women of the younger generation are no longer prepared to suffer such sexual harassment in silence.

> Two of our students had been molested by a group of twenty boys in a bus, and the conductor and driver had not co-operated by stopping immediately or taking action. That came out as a newspaper item; and then the whole college got very exercised about it and just went onto the roads and blocked the traffic for a couple of hours. Everything became an upsurge at that point of things they had been tolerating for a much longer period. There is a treatment of women, especially if they are young, unmarried and unat-tached; something happens to the male on the road, and he really does not behave as a gentleman. There are degrees of this – you could call it violence, dis-regard, disrespect – which go a long way, and I think our students have felt this. But they're also becoming bolder; because by being a little more confident, you can become less of a victim, and that is what we have decided to do. Maybe we cannot change the outside world, but we can change our perception of it.

Lady Irwin students are, for the most part, sophisticated, urban girls; but the battle for women's rights is also being taken up among the poor. Ela Bhatt points out that working-class women are often the major breadwinners in the family.

> In the case of a woman in a poor family, almost all the money that she earns goes into the expenses of the family, for food, clothes and a roof mainly, and that improves the quality of life in the family. But in the case of men, I would say they give only 50 per cent of their earnings to the family. The rest they want to spend for a cup of tea or *bidis*[1] or liquor or a movie. In so many cases I've found, I would say 33 or 39 per cent, women are the sole supporters of the family.

Ela Bhatt believes it is of cardinal importance that working women gain some economic independence from their husbands; and to this end, she has started a special bank for women.

> Money is power, so it helps women tremendously when they have their own bank account, though they do not want to let it be disclosed to the men. In our bank, we have a whole big cabinet full of their pass-books, because they do not want to take them home. There are about 129 cases where women were saving with us, and then later they wanted to release their land, which was mortgaged to some big farmer. So that is how about 129 women became the owners of their land; and then they also wanted loans to develop agriculture on this land. This has created so much confidence in these women, and their men also have been supportive. But it has also created quite a stir among the officials at the block level. They have a typical middle-class attitude, and they instigate the women's husbands to come to us and say: 'How can she have the land when I'm living? Only a widow can have land in her name.' Of course, it does bring some conflict; but in any struggle, there is always going to be some conflict.

As women become aware of their economic muscle, they are

1 Cheap cigarettes made from rolled tobacco leaves.

93

also becoming more career-conscious. Dr Anandalakshmy, for instance, has been noticing a definite change of attitude among her students.

> In the last three years, our freshmen have been asking: 'If I take this option, then what job can I take?' They have started with the assumption that they will definitely be working. For most people, it would be a job for extra income and, for a large majority, for some satisfaction, something to do outside the home. For a small number who are very talented, this will be the one way of expressing yourself, and nothing would stop you. So there are degrees of commitment to a career. But certainly things have changed, and everybody says: 'You must be able to have a job, and you have to be qualified to have one, and you will try and combine it with marriage.'

One example of the new generation of women professionals is Kalpana Mehta of *Saheli*, who trained as an engineer. She complains that women still face serious discrimination at all levels in industry.

> While we have very progressive laws, like good provision of maternity leave, and all factories are supposed to run creches and child care centres, in reality women are just not hired in the organised sector. Whatever little vocational training is done for women is towards traditional skills. Where men are taught how to turn lathes, women are taught how to embroider and do textile design and things like that, which again restricts their job market. What is very strange is that, even in textiles and mining, where a lot of women were employed traditionally, with increasing mechanisation and automation, women have just got pushed out of those jobs.

Kalpana Mehta says that her own problems began at the technological institute where she trained.

> Even before I entered the college, my father said: 'Are

94

you sure you want to go in for this education, because even I wouldn't employ a woman engineer.' There has been quite a prejudice which makes women stay away from these colleges: entering a college which is so male-dominated, being the only woman in a big class, where you don't have any collegiate support to study, where you're the strange person out ... The problems ranged from quite trivial ones, like not being able to bunk classes without being noticed, to very serious ones of not finding good partners to do your workshop or other experiments with, because everybody teased those boys who wanted to team up with girls.

The career limitations on a woman engineer eventually persuaded Kalpana Mehta to drop the idea. 'You won't get a shop-floor job,' she complains. 'What you land up getting is a job in research and design. Just as many men aren't interested in research and design and want to go in for production or engineering, the same is the case with women. That's one main reason why I dropped out.'

While women undoubtedly continue to face discrimination in the job market, sex is a far lesser disadvantage than the poor educational facilities available to most Indians. Middle-class women like Kalpana Mehta do at least have the advantage of a modern, English-language education. But education in the village schools run by the state still uses old-fashioned methods of learning by rote. A typical example is the primary school in a prosperous and bustling village in the district of Raipur Rani near Delhi. The children are healthy and alert; and as the headmistress lined them up to recite a story, she explained that most of them do now go on to the secondary schools provided by the government. But the language of instruction is Hindi, while it is English that remains the medium of instruction in India's more prestigious universities. The Chairman of the Central Government's Board of Secondary Education is a Jesuit priest, Father Kunankal. He says that class and language barriers converge to ensure that students of the élite and expensive, privately run, English-medium schools enjoy far greater opportunities in life.

I consider India a divided country, and a very potent

instrument for division is education and the medium of education. It leads on to a better college, to better jobs, economic status, house and all that goes with it. It's like a conveyor belt; once you get on, you're on. There is a very strong vested interest that is keen on preserving this, because it is to their advantage not to allow too many people to get onto this conveyor. There is a lot of hope and effort also from others who are not on the conveyor belt to get onto it. That is why there is a tremendous proliferation of so-called English-medium schools. The very announcement that 'This is an English-medium school' attracts people. No matter what the quality or the competence of the teacher; it sells.

The base of education has expanded dramatically since independence. Nearly 90 per cent of Indian children are now enrolled in primary schools, while places in secondary schools have multiplied twenty times since 1947. But the present Education and Health Minister, Narasimha Rao, admits that this numerical expansion has often been achieved at the expense of quality.

While education has expanded phenomenally, the quality has not been maintained; and the social justice aspect also has not been implemented to the extent we wanted. The standard of schooling given in a tribal area, for instance, bears no relation to what is given in the cities of Bombay or Delhi. What we really have to do now in implementing the new policy is to see that educational opportunity of a comparable standard is offered to all people as far as possible. We can't just say that we have half a million schools; that's not enough. We must be able to say that in the village schools we have, say, two teachers in each school; we have a building for each school; a playing-field for each school; that we have at least one teacher who is a woman in each school. These are some of the specifications which have been determined in the new policy called Operation Blackboard.

One of the aims of the Government's Operation Blackboard is

to eradicate illiteracy. Literacy has risen from the abysmal figure of 9 per cent at independence to 36 per cent now; a massive increase when one considers the population explosion during the same period. But is literacy as crucial a touchstone of progress as we sometimes assume? Dr Anandalakshmy, Principal of Delhi's Lady Irwin College, points out that people who have not learned to read can be just as cultured as the literate.

> Earlier we had eradication of malaria, and then small-pox; now we have eradication of illiteracy. It's put into the same category as disease, and I think that's unfortunate for several reasons. In a place like Rajasthan, for instance, the literacy level of women is very low, but the level of culture can be very high. In a Western country, where everybody is literate, literacy really means knowing how to cope with the system. But being illiterate in an Indian village is a very different thing and does not mean stupidity or ignorance in the same fashion.

Dr Anandalakshmy argues that India, unlike the West, has a strong oral tradition of learning. One did not need to be literate to be a scholar of the ancient scriptures. This tradition, she argues, can be a valuable asset in modern life, especially among women who lack a formal education.

> We've done some work in villages, where I've come upon at least two or three women who were out-standingly competent in managing their own business. They were good entrepreneurs whom you would admire in any culture; and they didn't have the basic literacy skills. One was even lending and borrowing, buying grain wholesale, lending it out at points, and she had a large amount of information in her head. We couldn't trip her up on it. She had lent things to forty people, different amounts at different times, which were due back to her. Her brain was like a computer; but on a demographic profile, she would just come out as ignorant, illiterate and so on.

While Dr Anandalakshmy deplores the stigma of illiteracy, she agrees that literacy is an important instrument in gaining access to knowledge and power. According to Tara Ali Baig, it is also an essential aid to solving one of India's most urgent problems, the population explosion.

> Take a state like Kerala, which has 90 per cent literacy. That is where you have your lowest mortality rate and, although it's very largely Catholic, your lowest birth rate. This is a very interesting phenomenon. It shows that, when education is available to women, then change takes place. It's in backward states like Rajasthan that we still have child marriages, mass marriages of children, because a very peculiar thing takes place there. The families dare not change it, because if half the families were to obey the rules, the other half would get their children married off very young, and there wouldn't be husbands enough for the girls who've been left behind.

Mahatma Gandhi maintained that self-control was the best form of birth control. When independent India decided that family planning could not be left to Gandhian-style abstinence, it was thought that all that was needed was to provide adequate supplies of contraceptives. Advertisements appeared everywhere, urging parents: 'Two or three children, then stop.' Health workers offered people every known method of birth control – caps, coils, sheaths, sterilisation and the pill. It was called 'the cafeteria approach', with people expected to help themselves. The advertisements can still be seen, and the cafeterias are still open; but it is now realised that the problem requires more complex solutions.

Ignorance and illiteracy may be one cause of large families, but another is economics. Children who can be sent out to earn even a few rupees are an asset, not a liability, for poorer parents. Health care is another factor. Children guarantee their parents' security in old age and a safe passage into their next lives, since Hindus believe that their funeral rites must be performed by a son. Because infant mortality is still high in most rural areas, parents do not regard one or even two sons as a safe guarantee. Nevertheless, as Narasimha Rao proudly points out, public health, like education, has made major strides since independence, and many of the old scourges, which used to decimate whole villages, have been eradicated.

We have succeeded in eradicating smallpox and the plague. I remember, in my childhood, almost every alternate year, we had plague in Hyderabad. We used to go and live in camps, and visitation by these epidemics was a very common thing in those days. It was taken as a fact of life. In fact, we had permanent structures where people used to go; they were called plague camps. We don't have any plague camps today; we don't have any case of smallpox today. The number of deaths due to malaria has been brought down considerably. It used to be about a million in 1947; now it's a very much less figure. The infant mortality rate has come down dramatically, and expectation of life has gone up dramatically.

Much of India's progress in the social welfare field has been due not merely to the efforts of government, but to the vast voluntary movement that has sprung up. Most of the new voluntary groups are involved, not in Victorian works of charity, but in evolving and implementing relevant and imaginative schemes to help poor Indians make more of their lives. It is also significant that some of the most successful projects have been organised by women's groups. One example is an organisation called *Mobile Creches*, in which Dr Ananda-lakshmy of Lady Irwin College is active. Its aim, she says, is to set up temporary creches on building sites to look after the children of female construction workers.

Contrary to the standard ideal of a very antiseptic environment with very lovely cribs and so on, we try to recreate the setting in which the families themselves live. The cribs are just very simple, cloth hammocks, tied to a wooden frame, which is very sturdy and can be washed easily. Then the walls – we often get them decorated by the mothers with the same kinds of patterns with which they are familiar and which are very beautiful. We use small huts very similar to the huts they live in; otherwise we live in tents, or in the basement of a building just completed, or on the first floor of a building still being built.

The emphasis is on providing an environment which is cheerful and colourful, but inexpensive. Dr Anandalakshmy contrasts this with some of the creches she has visited in the West, where conditions are so sterile and formal that they become alien to a working-class environment. 'Our workers dress as simply as possible,' she says. 'They've learned the dialect that the women speak, so they can speak to them comfortably. Nothing costs a lot, but a lot of thinking has gone into it.'

Offering simple answers to simple needs, and Indian answers to Indian needs, these creches use the workers' traditional love of puppet theatre to reconcile their internecine quarrels.

There were two contractors working on the same site, and there were constant wrangles between the children of these two groups. We had centres in both of them; so one of the teachers thought of a way of bringing them together and created what is called a wedding of two puppets. One centre produced the bride and the other the bridegroom, including the palanquin in which they were carried and everything else. Everybody got into the act; and the parents started making *puris*[1] and *halwa*[2] for the wedding; and the contractor donated money, very much as he would for any other wedding. It was an exercise which the children enjoyed, making musical instruments and picking up the old songs. The bridegroom's party went to the bride's and picked her up and came back. In this process, they all became friends; and the minor skirmishes were the kind that happen in any Indian wedding, but nothing more than that. They really became friendly after that, with jokes about having married into each other's families. Since it worked so well, we tried that out wherever there were two contractors working, or where the children felt themselves to be different groups.

1 Puffed Indian bread.
2 Sweetmeats.

Perhaps the greatest strength of the voluntary movement, and especially women's organisations, in India is that they have found ways of reconciling tradition with the struggle for equal rights in a modern society. According to Ela Bhatt, the major achievement of the women's movement has been not so much in altering the material status of women as in improving their own and society's awareness of their needs and rights.

> I'm very proud to say that women, in the last ten years, have been slowly coming together. On this whole issue of rape, they have come together in different parts of the country and been able to bring amendments in the law on rape. In the case of dowry murders also, they have come together and been able to change the law. Then education – for the first time, when the Government was deciding a new policy for education, it has been made mandatory to bring in equality of women as one of the themes in education.

Ela Bhatt cites the current emphasis on women's development in government plans, with a separate ministry set up for this purpose, as evidence of change. Against these successes, she says, a major and continuing weakness of the women's movement is that it remains largely the preserve of urban and educated women and has yet to reach poorer, rural women. 'We do lack a common vision of the future,' she concedes, 'and because of that, we are not able to come to a common strategy. And if you don't have a commonly thought out strategy, you can't be successful.'

THE CONGRESS SUCCESSION

In December 1985, the Indian National Congress celebrated its centenary in Bombay. Founded by a group of affluent civil servants, merchants and Western-educated intellectuals to lobby the Raj for democratic reforms, the Congress became a mass movement by the 1920s, and eventually the ruling party of independent India. Apart from a brief two-and-a-half-year interlude, Congress and its leaders have monopolised India's central government. Nevertheless, India's present prime minister, Rajiv Gandhi, shocked the vast gathering at the centenary celebrations by attacking them for straying from the highmindedness of the independence struggle and becoming a party of power-brokers. Although the party elders resented this, they showed no sign of anger; they had grown accustomed to bowing to the will of the Nehru dynasty.

Rajiv Gandhi represents the fourth generation of what must be the longest-lived political dynasty of the twentieth century. Its founder was Rajiv's great-grandfather, Pandit Motilal Nehru, a prosperous and Westernised barrister who abandoned his practice to become one of the top leaders of Congress in the years after World War I. Pandit Motilal had his differences with Mahatma Gandhi, but one thing they agreed upon was that the future of Congress lay with Motilal's radical young son, Jawaharlal, the hero of the Indian left. It was as a result of their joint canvassing that Jawaharlal succeeded his father as President of Congress in 1930, at the very moment when the party adopted full independence as its goal. From then onwards, Jawaharlal Nehru, for all his socialist ideas, remained loyal to the Mahatma; and Gandhi, in turn, ensured that Nehru became India's first prime minister.

Even so, the two men did have a serious disagreement over the future of Congress. The Mahatma saw it as an independence movement which should be disbanded after it had achieved its aim. But Nehru insisted that Congress was the only institution with the deep roots in the villages which were essential if democracy was to survive and flower. Forty years on, it is those very roots which have dried up; and they have dried up because the Nehru dynasty has become like a great banyan tree, in the shade of which nothing grows.

Nehru's later years were dominated by the question, 'After Nehru who?', so difficult had it become to imagine Congress or India without his towering presence. One of the candidates on everyone's short-list was his daughter, Indira Gandhi,[1] who was already a prominent Congress leader in her own right, having served as party president. But was it really the intention of India's democratic first prime minister to found a dynasty? Morarji Desai, one of the disappointed candidates for the succession, insists that it was. Shortly before Nehru died, he introduced what was called the Kamaraj Plan to revitalise the Congress Party. It required Morarji and some other senior ministers to leave their government posts and dedicate themselves to party work. Morarji Desai still maintains that the real aim of this exercise was to get rid of him and clear the road to power for Mrs Gandhi. But Nehru's sister, Vijayalakshmi Pandit, denies that he had any such dynastic ambitions. 'My brother,' she firmly maintains, 'had no idea that Indira would succeed him, nor did he think in terms of dynasty.' The Kamaraj Plan, she argues, was a necessary cleansing operation: 'People were sticking on, and it gave them an opportunity to go with self-respect.'

If Nehru did hope to pass on the succession to his only child, he certainly chose a very odd way to go about it. The dismissal of Morarji Desai and other senior ministers cleared the way, not for Mrs Gandhi, but for Nehru's loyal follower, Lal Bahadur Shastri, who was brought back into the Cabinet. When Nehru died in 1964, Indira Gandhi stayed out of the running, and it was Shastri who succeeded him. Mrs Gandhi's

[1] Her husband, Feroze Gandhi, was an active back-bench Congress M.P. and no relation to the Mahatma.

opportunity came a year and a half later when Shastri died suddenly of a heart attack; but Nehru could hardly have foreseen that.

On the face of it, Shastri was an odd choice to succeed a man of Nehru's stature. Physically, he was so small that he was known as 'The Little Sparrow'. Very much a local boy made good, he had none of the polish that Nehru's Western education had given him. India loves a royal family; and there was nothing regal about Shastri. Indira Gandhi was one of those who did not trouble to hide the fact that she thought Shastri unworthy to step into her father's shoes. But she was too ambitious to risk losing the limelight; and to some people's surprise, she agreed to serve in his Cabinet.

One of those who had reason to be puzzled by Mrs Gandhi's inconsistency in this regard was her aunt, Mrs Pandit. She recalls travelling with her niece on the ceremonial train which took Nehru's ashes to his home city of Allahabad to be scattered on the Ganges. As the train made its way slowly through vast crowds, the Nehru women discussed the political future.

> I said to Indira: 'I hope you're not going to accept a ministership, because it would be too soon. It would be much better if you went on working as you were in your father's time, and then came in. They have to have you.' She said: 'You're quite right, and I wouldn't.' The next day I turned on the radio at 8 o'clock in the morning, and the first announcement was: 'Mrs Gandhi has accepted'. She was in the room with me, and she said: 'There's some misunderstanding. I'll speak to him about it.' But there never was any misunderstanding. He had to have a Nehru, and she was obviously the choice at that moment.

It is a measure of the extent to which Congress has become the Nehru family party that Shastri is now virtually unremembered. The cheerleaders who warm up party meetings shout: 'Jai [long live] Mahatma Gandhi, Jawaharlal Nehru, Indira Gandhi, Rajiv Gandhi'. Shastri is conveniently missed out. But it was Shastri, during his eighteen-month rule, who steered India through one of its gravest crises, the second war with Pakistan in 1965. L. K. Jha headed the Prime Minister's

Secretariat under both Shastri and Mrs Gandhi, and he is full of praise for the way that Shastri overcame the limitations of his background.

> He suffered from some feeling of inferiority complex; being successor to Nehru was not an easy thing. He was also conscious that he hadn't studied English too well. In fact, he had educated himself in the English language by reading the works of Bertrand Russell in jail. The first time he went to England as Prime Minister, he asked to meet Russell. Harold Wilson said: 'We'll arrange for him to come and see you.' But Shastri said: 'Not on your life. I must go to him.' So he went to call on his guru, Bertrand Russell. He was not very articulate in these matters, but he had a very deep feeling of empathy with the kind of things which Russell was talking about.
> When it came to the Indo-Pakistan conflict, I found him extremely good. He gave full authority to a group of secretaries[1] to take decisions on all issues at all times. He himself had an emergency committee of the Cabinet, over which he used to preside. It used to meet very frequently even at short notice, sometimes late in the night, to deal with all matters of importance. And he did not hesitate to clear the idea that the Indian army could march towards Lahore,[2] because you couldn't fight a localised war in Kashmir without being handicapped.

Although Shastri conducted the war vigorously, he had the courage to accept ceasefire terms which he knew would be unpopular in India. He died immediately after signing that ceasefire agreement. Mrs Gandhi, by this time, was well poised to succeed him. Although she had held the relatively unimportant post of Minister for Information in Shastri's Cabinet, a combination of personal courage and shrewd political timing had won her the sexist but flattering title of 'The Only Man in the Cabinet'. The veteran journalist, Romesh Thapar, then a close confidant of hers, has described how she upstaged

1 Permanent heads of government departments.
2 Capital of the Punjab province of West Pakistan.

Shastri when violent rioting broke out in the south against the imposition of the Hindi language by the central government.

> She had a little consultation with me and a few others. I told her: 'You should go to the south and say: "Over my dead body will Hindi be forced down your throats".' And before I knew what had happened, she'd caught the evening flight to Madras and delivered a statement. By the next morning, she was a national figure looked up to in the south and the north as somebody who has *dum* or courage. She had that quality always. During the Indo-Pakistan War, when Shastri was Prime Minister, she was there on the Kashmir front, flying in on special aircraft, taking an interest in everything, visiting the front. When there was a communal riot in the Delhi area, she would go personally in a jeep and start parading herself there, so that everybody slunk away, knowing she would descend on them. It was this kind of personalised leadership and courage which really brought her up in a phenomenal way.

Nevertheless, the party old guard who chose Indira Gandhi as Shastri's successor did not think much of her qualities of leadership. They chose her because they believed that her lack of experience would make her clay in their skilled hands. At first they seemed to be right, because the woman who later came to be described as the Empress of India made a very hesitant start. L. K. Jha, who continued as principal secretary under the new prime minister, remembers her early days in office.

> She was unsure of herself, because she had got elected with a very strong challenge from Morarji Desai, and a lot of the party members would have preferred him. More important, her party itself was not in a tremendously strong position, and the Opposition was very, very strong. Then, she did not have enough self-confidence to be able to make an extempore speech; she had to prepare a text; and the Opposition, knowing that she was speaking from a text, would try to interrupt

her. But the speed with which she picked up was quite impressive. Once she began to gain in political strength, then all her other abilities blossomed forth.

But according to N. K. Seshan, the private secretary she inherited from Nehru, Mrs Gandhi could never hold a candle to her father, at least as far as parliamentary skills were concerned.

He used to respect Parliament. He used to be in Parliament punctually on the dot. Every day, at 11am he used to be in the House. Whenever any important debates came, he would be personally present. He would intervene, support, take decisions on the spot. Sometimes he would find that the Opposition's viewpoint was correct, and he would agree to their viewpoint on the floor of the House. This could be done only because the Prime Minister was present in the House. But Mrs Gandhi used to avoid any major debate in the House. She was unable to handle the situation in Parliament, whereas he was a great parliamentarian.

Seshan blames Mrs Gandhi's inexperience for some of the early blunders of her government.

I don't think she had a clue of how to rule a country of 600 million people. Unlike Panditji [Nehru], who was a great man with vision and ideas, Mrs Gandhi had to rely on her so-called advisers. They are the people who forced her to devalue the rupee at the behest of the World Bank. I do not think, left to herself, she would have devalued. I do not think she ever realised the implications of devaluation.

The decision to devalue the rupee also devalued Mrs Gandhi's political rating. She took a bad knock in the 1967 general election, with the Congress majority at the Centre drastically reduced and the Opposition winning power in all the states along the Gangetic plain. The party bosses or 'Syndicate', as they were called, decided that the time had come to clip her wings by nominating their own candidate in the election for the President of India. The Prime Minister and her small group of advisers reckoned that it would be better to take the offensive and split the party rather than accept the Syndicate's nominee. The Indian President, in theory at least, had the constitutional right to dismiss a prime minister; and Mrs Gandhi was not going to take any risks.

In the battle that ensued, she managed to outmanoeuvre the veterans who used to dismiss her as 'yesterday's *bacha* [child]'. Romesh Thapar, then a member of what became known as her kitchen-cabinet, says that the Congress split of 1970 brought out the best in her.

> She was a transformed character, and I realised suddenly her basic strength: she knew every Congressman, his relationships, his compromises in the past. She knew exactly how to place them, how they would vote. I remember various colleagues of hers saying: 'These four certainly, Indiraji, will support us.' And she said: 'Well, two of them won't, and I'll tell you why.' She gave a detailed explanation, and the chap was silent. She was a human computer where the Congress Party was concerned.

Mrs Gandhi was far too shrewd a politician to think that winning the battle within the party was enough. She knew she had to take the people with her and recover the ground the undivided Congress had lost. Realising that she had no ideological clothes, the empress donned red robes. It was a clever move, because Morarji Desai and the old guard could never sell themselves as socialists. The two most controversial populist measures she took were to nationalise the banks and to strip the Indian princes of the privileges and privy purses guaranteed to them by her father.

After introducing these measures and putting her opponents on the defensive, Mrs Gandhi called an early general election. Her main slogan was *Garibi Hatao* ('Eradicate Poverty'), and the electorate responded to it by sending her opponents into the political wilderness and giving her a two-thirds majority in Parliament. The 1971 general election marks the arrival of the Indira Gandhi who is now remembered. The charming but easily flustered political *ingénue* was replaced by an imperious leader who would brook no opposition. One of those who fell victim to her new ways was her former Foreign Minister and confidant, Dinesh Singh. He had cause to regret the difference in political style between Mrs Gandhi and her father. 'She was more authoritarian, and she took decisions by herself,' he explains. 'Mr Nehru took his decisions in consultation with others. He was very democratic in his functioning as prime minister, and Mrs Gandhi was just the opposite.' Dinesh Singh says that he can only guess at the reasons for his own fall from favour.

> I could never find out from Mrs Gandhi, although I asked her several times on different occasions. I think what went wrong was a change in the style of functioning. She had got into a position where she felt that the relationship with her Cabinet colleagues should be more or less a master-slave relationship; and I always felt that the relations should be on the basis of two colleagues. I had a long talk with her and tried to tell her that, while I was completely loyal to her and the party, I did not feel I had any role left in government as such. At that time she did not agree, because she said elections were coming, and if I went there would be doubts created. So I did not press my resignation. But later on, she felt it was no longer necessary to have me in the government, because by then she had built up a new team.

Mrs Gandhi's electoral triumph was followed by an event which finally established her supremacy, the defeat of the Pakistan army in East Pakistan and the creation of the new state of Bangladesh. The crisis in Pakistan's eastern wing started with a brutal military crackdown against Bengali nationalism by the country's military ruler, General Yahya Khan. The break-up of Pakistan was probably inherent in a state divided by geography and strong regional differences, with religion and military force as its only unifying agents. But for Mrs Gandhi, it was an opportunity to assert India's dominance in the sub-continent and cut Pakistan down to size. She appeared to move with skill and certainty towards the war which was necessary to achieve those aims, neutralising America by signing a treaty of friendship with the Soviet Union.

Yet, there is evidence to suggest that, almost till the end, Mrs Gandhi hoped that war could be avoided and that the Americans would use their influence with Pakistan to create conditions in which the millions of Bengali refugees who had fled to India could return home.

Romesh Thapar met her just before she set out for Washington to persuade President Nixon to see her side of the argument. Her main concern, she told him, was the impact that the presence of 10 million refugees from East Pakistan was having on communal harmony in India. Unless the refugees returned soon, she feared that Hindu chauvinist groups would exploit the situation to unleash reciprocal violence against Indian Muslims. 'She went with that kind of fear to Nixon,' says Thapar, 'and she really believed that she could persuade him to curb Pakistan, to arrange a kind of clean-up of its policies in Bangladesh, and perhaps achieve this through a peaceful initiative.'

Her pleas seem to have fallen on deaf ears in Washington. Thapar, who was there himself on a private visit, heard her addressing a public meeting at Washington Cathedral. The anger and frustration in her voice revealed that her mission had failed. 'I heard her speak,' he recalls, 'and I turned round to my wife and said: "It's war".'

L. K. Jha was by then India's Ambassador in Washington and played an important part in Mrs Gandhi's talks at the White House. He attributes the failure of the talks to a personal and long-standing prejudice against India.

The real opposition to the Indian standpoint came from President Nixon. My own feeling is – and I have had some very high-level Americans saying it to me – that it dates back to the time he came to India after losing his bid for presidentship to Kennedy. Jawaharlal Nehru thought that the best person to play host to him would be Morarji Desai, because he was number two in the Cabinet and also, on the whole, friendly to the Americans. But Morarji Desai is not a terribly good host. He gave Nixon a dry, vegetarian dinner; and to him it looked as if he was being treated very shabbily, in deep contrast to the kind of welcome he got when he went to Pakistan. There he was greeted as the architect of the Alliance and toasted and wined and dined. This left him with a feeling of rancour, that somehow the Indians were pro-Kennedy and anti-him personally.

He also had the feeling that the alliance with Pakistan had to be honoured; and there was a deeper factor, shared by both Kissinger and Nixon. They had developed a relationship with China; and they felt that China would judge America in terms of what America did for Pakistan. So if they were seen to be standing up for Pakistan very vigorously, then American–Chinese solidarity would really be strengthened.

In the event, it was Pakistan which finally sparked off the war by attempting a preemptive air-strike on the western front. The fighting lasted just twelve days, and Mrs Gandhi received an uproarious ovation when she announced its end in the Indian Parliament. 'The West Pakistan forces have unconditionally surrendered,' she shouted above the cheers. 'Dacca is now the free capital of a free country.' Not only had she given India its first military victory, but she had cocked a snook at the gunboat diplomacy of the world's leading superpower. Although President Nixon stopped short of direct military intervention on Pakistan's side, he did send the American Seventh Fleet into the Bay of Bengal. 'I personally felt convinced,' recalls L. K. Jha, 'that American public opinion would not stand for another front in Asia being opened up by the Americans. But the naval presence was meant to frighten India and to signal to China that "Look, we are quite ready to take firm action". But Indira Gandhi was totally firm, and she did not get deflected on account of the movement of the Seventh Fleet.'

Nixon's support for Pakistan in the war was to leave a permanent scar on Mrs Gandhi; and she never again trusted Washington. The Americans, for their part, wrote her off as a Soviet stooge. She did value India's special relationship with the Soviet Union, trusting the Kremlin to act as a bulwark against American and Chinese ambitions. But she was nobody's stooge, according to Inder Gujral, who served both

Mrs Gandhi and her opponents of the Janata Government as Ambassador in Moscow.

> Whatever else one may say about Mrs Gandhi's policies at home, I think in foreign affairs she was excellent. She had a very good assessment of Indo-Soviet relations. Sometimes people were uncharitable to her, as if the Soviets had influence on her; but I don't believe it. Mrs Gandhi was so conscious of our national interest and the safeguarding of it that she did it with remarkable finesse. For instance, she never accepted the desirability of the Soviets entering Afghanistan. She did not come out to criticise them openly, not because she was beholden to the Soviet Union, but because of the American policy in Pakistan. I was privy to this, that Mrs Gandhi had told the Russians in categorical language that she could never approve of their entry into Afghanistan. Mrs Gandhi always held her ground on essentials; and the Soviet leaders respected her a great deal, because they knew they could not take her for granted.

In the immediate aftermath of the Bangladesh War, the Russians were not the only ones to respect Mrs Gandhi. Pakistan's crushing defeat and the creation of independent Bangladesh seemed at one stroke to have redressed much of the harm done by partition, while wiping the slate clean of India's humiliating defeat in the China War. Indira Gandhi may have lacked her father's moral or intellectual stature; but Nehru never enjoyed the power or prestige his daughter did at the end of 1971, crowned with such decisive electoral and military victory within the short space of a year. The Congress Party, the country and the sub-continent were at her feet; but unfortunately she forgot the famous maxim that 'All power corrupts, and absolute power corrupts absolutely'.

DYNASTIC DEMOCRACY

Many of those who supported Mrs Gandhi in her battles with the Congress old guard and with Pakistan's military dictatorship were later to discover that the woman who had seemed to represent her father's humane and liberal political vision could herself be ruthless and autocratic in power. 1971 was to mark the end of collective leadership and internal democracy within Congress; they were replaced by the personality cult of an undisputed leader. R. K. Hegde, one of India's most respected Opposition leaders today, attributes this, not only to Mrs Gandhi's wishes, but to India's long-standing tradition of deifying its leaders.

> Indian people have a weakness for those who make sacrifices. During the freedom struggle, in the case of leaders like Mahatma Gandhi and Jawaharlal Nehru, it was also to some extent leader-oriented. It cannot be programme-oriented or ideology-oriented, because the vast majority of our people are illiterate. So the only motivating factor would be an individual who can mobilise their opinion and give them some kind of identity. This got an added significance during Mrs Gandhi's rule, because she wanted to make up her deficiencies by boosting her own image. She suffered from an inferiority complex; and she always had a feeling that she was not equal to the job. Her problem was that she was unable to reconcile her ambition and her deficiencies.

Mrs Gandhi certainly placed a far greater reliance on image-politics than any of her predecessors. The most alarming development for many of her own supporters was that the cult of personality began to take on an increasingly dynastic flavour. A sure indication of this was the growing influence of her younger son, Sanjay, which led to serious disagreements between Mrs Gandhi and her principal secretary, P. N. Haksar, a man widely respected for his integrity and intellect. Haksar, more than anyone else, had guided her through the difficult days of the party split and the Bangladesh war. But according to N. K. Seshan, who was the Prime Minister's private secretary, her indulgence of Sanjay eventually led to Haksar's resignation. 'Sanjay was given a free hand,' says Seshan, 'and he was totally irresponsible. But she never used to curb him. In the beginning, she used to shout at him, but later she didn't bother at all about it. Haksar did not approve of Sanjay's activities at all.'

According to Seshan, Haksar tried hard to warn Mrs Gandhi about the damage her son was doing and even tried to persuade her with an analogy from the Hindu epic, the *Ramayana*. The hero, Lord Rama, he pointed out to her, had been sent into exile for fourteen years by his father, so that he could prove himself; and he had returned in triumph. He went on to suggest that she send Sanjay for three years to Kashmir to stop him interfering. But as it turned out, it was Haksar, not Sanjay, she chose to dispense with.

Sanjay was a brash and self-confident young man whose lack of educational achievement had left him with a deep-seated scorn for ideas and a passion for action. He did not qualify to go to university, and so was sent to Rolls Royce Cars in Britain as an apprentice. Although he never completed his apprenticeship, he returned to India and persuaded his mother to allow him to set up a plant to manufacture the first wholly Indian car. It was to be named *Maruti* or 'Son of the Wind God'.

The project bristled with controversies – over the allocation of this much sought after industrial licence to someone so inexperienced, over the grant of prime land on the outskirts of Delhi, over the finance, and over the product. Allegations of corruption caused an almost continuous uproar in Parliament and spilled into the press. Romesh Thapar, till then a friend and supporter of Mrs Gandhi's, was one of those who tried to warn her of the damage this was doing to her reputation.

> I began a series of collisions with Mrs Gandhi over all this corruption. She used to get very indignant and say: 'You know that I don't do anything like this, and it's absurd.' I said: 'Well, if you're not prepared to accept what people are feeling, then we'll call it a day.' 'No, no,' she said, 'I'm not saying that. I'm just saying that you must discipline yourself and think of all the problems I have to face.' So I said: 'Well, I'm just telling you that people think you're corrupt.' She said: 'I am not.' I said: 'They say you're the queen bee that sends them out to make the collection.' She was very upset, and so we started meeting less frequently. Frankly, she was getting adjusted to this new role of a kind of mafia queen.

Mrs Gandhi shut her ears to the advice of her more disinterested well-wishers and dismissed all allegations against her son as prejudice and exaggeration. 'She would just sit there ruminating,' Thapar complained, 'doing little doodles in silence. And then she would look up and ask another question which was a diversion.'

Mrs Gandhi once publicly replied to Sanjay's critics by saying: 'There is nothing wrong in a young man proving his capacity. His product will have to stand the test of the public.' But it never did, because there never was a product. Mrs Gandhi eventually asked the Japanese firm, Suzuki, to rescue *Maruti*; and the factory which was to have produced the first wholly Indian car ended up producing India's first wholly Japanese car instead.

By 1974, the *Maruti* controversy, raging inflation, and agitations against corruption had developed into a mass movement against the leader who had been so popular only two years earlier. Known as the J.P. movement, it was headed by Jayaprakash Narayan, or J.P. as he was popularly known, a veteran of the nationalist movement whom many regarded as the moral heir to Mahatma Gandhi. J.P. advocated non-violent civil disobedience on Gandhian lines to bring down the government; and his non-party crusade succeeded in attracting wide support from all sections of the political spectrum, including some of the Congress radicals who had formerly been close to Mrs Gandhi.

Realising that doubts were growing about her will to govern, the Prime Minister decided that she must take stern action to re-assert her authority. The first to feel her iron fist were the railway workers who launched a national strike in 1974. George Fernandes, the trade union leader who led the strike, explains why Mrs Gandhi, once the friend of the poor and dispossessed, was so keen to break it.

> The railways are really the lifeline of India, in terms of our economic activity. A prolonged railway strike would mean a shut-down of power-stations, would mean food-grains not reaching places where they are needed, would mean really the end of all economic activity. Therefore, while the strike was essentially on very simple economic issues, she saw in this a political challenge, and she felt that it must be put down. So the response from her was absolutely ferocious. Both the Railway Minister and the Chairman of the Railway Board had cautioned me: 'Your demands are right, but we are under pressure and there is nothing we can do, because Mrs Gandhi has a different attitude to this.' Looking at the way she suppressed the strike, my reaction was that it was a kind of dress-rehearsal for a fascist takeover of this country.

While showing the railway workers who was boss, Mrs Gandhi also tried to refurbish her image as a decisive leader by ordering Indian scientists to explode a nuclear device. But within a year, a major political bomb had exploded in her own face when the High Court in her home city of Allahabad found her guilty of corrupt electoral practices. The charges were largely technical, but the verdict was a godsend for the Opposition who demanded that she resign. Fearing that even a temporary resignation was too risky in the prevailing political climate, a small group of her advisers, including Sanjay, persuaded Mrs Gandhi to proclaim a state of emergency instead and crack down hard on her opponents.

'The President has proclaimed emergency,' the Prime Minister announced in her broadcast to a stunned nation. 'This is nothing to panic about. I'm sure you are all conscious of the deep and widespread conspiracy which has been brewing ever since I began introducing certain progressive measures of benefit to the common man and woman of India.'

To the common man and woman, it seemed as if the only panic had been in Mrs Gandhi's own inner circle. She claimed that she had acted to forestall a right-wing conspiracy; but most Indians interpreted the Emergency as a bid to save the ruling dynasty. That was hardly surprising when the sub-servient president of the Congress Party endorsed the Emergency with the immortal words: 'India is Indira, and Indira is India'. The Opposition leaders and their active supporters were arrested; and the BBC's Delhi correspondent almost ended up with them, thanks to Mohammed Yunus, a close family friend of the Prime Minister's, who held no office but wielded considerable power. Believing that the BBC had broadcast that some members of the Government were not supporting the Emergency and had been put under house arrest, Yunus ordered Mark Tully's arrest. Fortunately, the then Information Minister, Inder Gujral, persuaded Mrs Gandhi that it was all a mistake.

The day the Emergency came in, that evening I was sitting at home and Yunus telephoned me and said: 'The BBC has said that Jagjivan Ram, Swaran Singh,[1] yourself and one or two others are under house arrest. You send for Mark Tully, pull down his trousers, give him a few lashes and send him to jail.' I said: 'Look Yunus, this is not my job. This is a job for the Home Minister; so you talk to him, not to me.' Immediately after I'd put down the phone, I sent for the monitoring report of the BBC, and the BBC had not said it. So I spoke to the PM and said: 'Yunus has just told me this. I have seen the monitoring report, and I'm sending it to you.' Subsequently, in the evening when we met, I drew her attention to this and asked: 'Did you see the monitoring report?' She said: 'Yes, I have seen it. But he said he heard that. Maybe he heard some other radio.'

1   Senior members of the Government.

Today Inder Gujral can chuckle as he remembers the hysteria of those days. But imprisonment was not a pleasant experience for those who were unable to avoid arrest. One of them was George Fernandes, the labour leader, who was trying to organise an underground, sabotage campaign against the Emergency.

> I was brought to Delhi and driven straight to the Red Fort, where I was put in a dungeon. The first thing they did was to strip me of all my clothes. I had nothing to wear, and they gave me a blanket on which to sleep. It was June 1976, the height of summer in Delhi; and in that dungeon, there was no question of fans or any kind of comforts. A coarse blanket was spread out, and I was asked to lie on that. For part of the day, I used to be taken into a very small cubicle, where one knew there were a number of eyes that were watching you from somewhere beyond. You were sitting on a stool, and there were a couple of officials who kept asking questions, who threatened to beat but never beat me. Their fight against me was more psychological, the way they interrogated me.

Fernandes was particularly roughly treated because he had advocated violent resistance to the government. But even a committed, non-violent Gandhian like Morarji Desai, though treated with civility, had to endure several months of solitary confinement. Morarji, who prides himself on always making the best of a bad situation, looks back with some satisfaction on those days of confinement. 'I was not allowed to go out of my room,' he recalls, 'but it didn't bother me. I began to walk in my room, and that practice enables me even now to take my walk without going out. I always utilise things like that for the better.' Although he was allowed no companions or visitors, he decided to make the most of the company of the policemen who guarded him.

> The police came and talked to me about their problems, and I helped them. That's why they respected me and somehow had a great attraction for me. They told me: 'You are going to be Prime Minister, and then the

country will be all right.' No papers were allowed to me, but they used to give me all the information.

Another illustrious prisoner who decided to make the best of her situation was the redoubtable Rajmata (Queen Mother) of Gwalior, a leader of the right-wing, Hindu opposition party. When she heard that there was a warrant out for her arrest, she decided to go underground and hid herself in the Delhi homes of various friends. Later, to avoid government harassment of her children, she gave herself up to the police at the family palace in Gwalior. She was transferred to Delhi's top security jail, in the company of women criminals and prostitutes.

> There were no sanitary arrangements, so they used to do their business in the open drains, and it was stinking like hell. All that I had to go through, but I was determined that I was not going to be cowed down by any sort of harassment. I realised that they were doing this to make me surrender, so I said: 'No, I'm going to keep myself in good cheer and show them that it's not going to affect me.' And these inmates of the jail – I used to sit and talk to them, try to probe and find out what their life was like, why they became criminals and prostitutes.

Outside the jails, the Emergency sought to justify itself with all the usual palaver of a Third World coup. It was as if India had become a banana republic. Mrs Gandhi and the Indian press, now controlled by strict censorship, lashed out at the corrupt, the blackmarketeers, the inefficient and the idle; and they promised a government that worked. According to Inder Gujral, then Information Minister in Mrs Gandhi's government, it was clear from the very first Cabinet meeting after the declaration of Emergency that Sanjay Gandhi was calling the shots.

> Sanjay's takeover was very visible immediately after the Cabinet. As we came out of the room, he was standing there. He walked over to me and said: 'I want to see the All India Radio news bulletins.' I said: 'Yes, it is a public document. You can see it.' 'No, no,' he said, 'I want to see them before they're broadcast.' So I

said: 'No, that is neither desirable nor feasible.' Since I had slightly raised my voice, Mrs Gandhi, who was standing nearby, came over and asked: 'What is the matter?' 'He wants to see the bulletins,' I said, 'and he can't.'

When I came home in the family we decided that I must get out [of the Government]. As chance would have it, an hour or so later, a telephone call came from the Prime Minister's house asking me to go there before going to my office. By the time I reached the Prime Minister's house, she had left. But as I was leaving, Sanjay came in and said: 'No, I want to talk to you.' And he spoke to me rudely about the Prime Minister's broadcast not having been carried by all channels of All India Radio. So I hit back and told him: 'If you ever want to talk to me, you will learn to be civil and polite; and you will not talk to me about government matters. I am not accountable to you.' I came back home and told my wife: 'Now I won't have to formally resign. I think it's been done!'

At first, Sanjay succeeded in terrorising India's notoriously lethargic bureaucracy into action. But it was not long before they found that the Emergency gave them even greater opportunities than before to line their pockets. They simply asked for bigger bribes, because they said the punishment for getting caught was more serious. Unfortunately, the chances of getting caught did not markedly increase. As for the police, they revelled in their almost unlimited powers of arrest. Sanjay Gandhi had given them a free hand to implement his controversial programmes of slum clearance and sterilisation.

As the Emergency entered its second year, some of Mrs Gandhi's own more enlightened supporters argued that it should be called off now that the immediate crisis had passed. One of them was B. K. Nehru, the Prime Minister's cousin, who had the difficult job of justifying the Emergency abroad as High Commissioner in London.

I would still defend the Emergency. I think it was the correct thing to do when it was done; but it went on far too long. An emergency is a short-term affair; it is meant to correct a particular situation. If the elections had taken place when they were due, in January 1976, Mrs Gandhi would have come back with a fantastic majority, because the Emergency was then so popular. Instead of that it went on and on and on; and with all kinds of unrestricted power, it naturally deteriorated.

Why did an astute politician like Mrs Gandhi ignore such advice? Girilal Jain, one of the few senior Indian journalists who remained sympathetic to her, offers some explanations.

Indira Gandhi was always very defensive on two subjects – the Emergency and Sanjay Gandhi. It was not possible for anyone to discuss Sanjay objectively with her; and it was also not possible to press questions on the Emergency, unless one was prepared for a break of relations. I saw no point in breaking relations, such as they were, with her. But people very close to her – members of her Secretariat who enjoyed her confidence and people who were her personal friends – any number of them have told me that she wanted to lift the censorship, if not the Emergency, around 15 August 1975.[1] But on that day, Sheikh Mujibur Rahman, President of Bangladesh, was massacred with members of his family, and Indira Gandhi then became very apprehensive about her own future. She had no doubt that external agencies had been responsible for the killing of Sheikh Mujib, and she was convinced they would do the same to her if she allowed power to slip out of her hands. There were others in her entourage who played on these fears to continue the Emergency.

Although she retained the Emergency and seemed to many observers to be preparing the ground for a dynastic dictatorship, Mrs Gandhi remained reluctant to jettison altogether the democratic forms to which her father had attached so much importance. 'The ghost of Jawaharlal Nehru haunted her,' says Girilal Jain. 'Indira Gandhi sought legitimacy in being

1 Indian Independence Day.

seen as not only the daughter but legitimate successor to Nehru, which meant sticking at least to the forms, if not the substance, of democracy.'

This ambivalence probably explains why Mrs Gandhi took the extraordinary step of calling a general election in February 1977, at a time when the Emergency, still in force, was at its most unpopular. Her former confidant, Dinesh Singh, thinks that the bureaucracy and intelligence agencies were responsible for advising her to make what proved a monumental political blunder.

> It was certainly not Sanjay, because he was not in favour of elections then. We [in the Congress Party] were not in favour of elections at that time. We said that you must first withdraw the Emergency, release the prisoners and give us six months to re-establish a rapport with the electorate. I can't imagine any politician having advised her to hold elections at that time.

What did the most damage to Mrs Gandhi in the election campaign were the allegations of forcible mass sterilisations throughout northern India. There were instances of unmarried, young men, and also old men in their seventies, who claimed that they had been forced to undergo this operation by Sanjay's over-zealous followers. In many places, villagers said that they used to hide *en masse* in the fields whenever officials arrived, in case they had come to sterilise them.

Sanjay, for his part, maintained that such panic was based on nothing more than unfounded rumours. 'In my own constituency,' he told the BBC, 'there's a lot of propaganda about sterilisation. I've asked people in every meeting if they can produce someone who has been forcibly sterilised; and the only answer I get is: "We have heard about it, but it's not happened here."'

Although Sanjay and his mother dismissed all the horror stories about the Emergency as Opposition propaganda, they could not escape evidence of the ugly mood among the electorate, especially in northern India. Mrs Gandhi herself encountered it at her first election meeting in Delhi. The crowd sat solemn and silent as she screamed accusations against her opponents. When she realised it was all to no avail, she ran down from the rostrum and scrambled over a fence into the crowd to appeal directly for their support. She was pulled back by her security men. As the election campaign developed, she had to face many more such hostile audiences; but she fought on regardless and refused to accept defeat. 'I am never fearful,' she assured David Dimbleby of the BBC, 'because I don't do things for success or failure, and I'm not really concerned about praise or blame. I do what I think I have to do for the country. And I have to use every ounce of strength to strengthen the base of this country, so that cannot be destroyed.'

The election campaign also demonstrated that the ruling dynasty itself was divided, with the Prime Minister's aunt campaigning openly on the other side. Mrs Vijayalakshmi Pandit came out of retirement at a dramatic press conference organised by the Opposition. There she poured scorn on her niece for seeking votes in the name of the sacrifices her family had made for India. Mrs Pandit still remembers it as one of the most satisfying moments of her long life.

> It was a wonderful occasion for me, because I was able to say so many things I'd always wanted to. One of them was that I was sick and tired of hearing that the Nehrus had made the biggest sacrifices. I've never thought that, because a sacrifice is something you make by giving up something. What did we give up? We gave up money. Well, that was all right; we gave it up because we wanted to do something else. My brother always said: 'If I had not given that up, that would have been a sacrifice.' I remember someone asked me: 'Do you believe that the Nehrus made the greatest sacrifice?' I said: 'If they did, they've been paid for it.' Indira didn't like this at all. She rang me up that night and said: 'Phupi,[1] did you say this?' I said: 'I'm afraid I did.' 'Do you think it's right?' she asked. I said: 'Well, don't you think it's right? My brother was all these years in power; you succeeded him; I've been in big positions; three-quarters of it was because I was a Nehru.'

Mrs Gandhi may not have approved of her aunt's denial of the

1 Auntie.

divine right of the Nehrus to rule India; but she did bow gracefully enough to the verdict of the electorate. The Congress Party was routed in its traditional stronghold of northern India, and the Prime Minister and her son suffered the ultimate humiliation of losing their own seats by large margins. 'My colleagues and I accept the verdict unreservedly and in a spirit of humility,' Mrs Gandhi announced in a farewell broadcast to the nation. 'Elections are part of the democratic process to which we are deeply committed. I have always said, and I do believe, that the winning or losing of an election is less important than the strengthening of our country and ensuring a better life for our people. I give my good wishes to the new government that will be formed.'

The new government was formed by the Janata Party, a shot-gun marriage of various non-Communist opposition parties, with some dissident Congressmen added for good measure. The marriage had taken place with the blessings of the ailing but revered Jayaprakash Narayan as soon as the Opposition leaders were released from jail, and it was held together by the pressures of an immediate election campaign. Mrs Gandhi's greatest mistake was that she did not defer elections until Janata's internal contradictions had time to surface. If the Opposition leaders had been given more time to argue about the division of seats, about their status within the new party, and perhaps even about policy, Janata might not have got to the starting gate.

Although she never apologised for the Emergency, Mrs Gandhi seems to have realised that she should have heeded the counsel of the few advisers who had been frank enough to give her unpopular advice. Inder Gujral, who was dismissed as Information Minister because he opposed censorship, says that Mrs Gandhi later thanked him for his candour in her moment of defeat.

> When she was defeated and I went to meet her, it was a very touching meeting. She was sitting there with her luggage packed. She was going to move house, and there was a drop of a tear in her eye. Voluntarily, without my provoking anything, she said: 'Yes, you told me so.'

No sooner had the Janata Party achieved the unthinkable by

defeating Mrs Gandhi, than its temporary unity started to fall apart. A row broke out over who should become prime minister which Jayaprakash Narayan settled by nominating the octogenarian Morarji Desai, a seasoned administrator, but too rigid to be an effective party leader. George Fernandes, Minister for Industry in the new government, thinks it might have held together better if there had been an open contest for the leadership, even though the victor would probably have been the *Harijan* politician, Jagjivan Ram, who had only recently defected from Congress.

> If we had gone through the process of a democratic election of our leader, it would have made a world of difference to the Janata Party, and I don't think the party would have gone down the way it did. Morarji, for all his virtues and good qualities, and I think as Prime Minister he led the team in the best possible manner that he could, was always hamstrung by this attack – that he was leader because somebody willed that he should be leader. And someone else harboured the feeling that he could have been leader, but was not allowed to be. Perhaps, in the circumstances, Jagjivan Ram would have been a much better man to lead for a number of reasons, including the fact that he belonged to the Scheduled Castes.[1] Having him as prime minister would have demolished this myth that wisdom is inherited from father to daughter to son to grandchildren and is only available in Kashmir.[2]

Despite this starting handicap, Fernandes insists that the Janata Government was no mere stop-gap.

> The Janata Government was the best government this country has had. I am not saying this because I happened to be a member of that government. I am quoting a man who saw all governments since independence and finally retired as Cabinet Secretary, the topmost civil servant in the country – Mr Nirmal Mukherji – a man who has sat in on more Cabinet

1 Underprivileged, lower castes listed in the Indian Constitution for special provision.
2 The region where the Nehru family originated.

meetings than perhaps any civilian in this country. His view was that this was the best and most talented government, and perhaps the most honest and open government, the country has had.

Among the achievements of Janata rule, Fernandes cites new economic policies aimed at promoting decentralised industries at the district level, excellent relations with India's smaller neighbours, a liberal attitude to minorities, and above all the restoration of the civil liberties so drastically curtailed during the Emergency. Despite such successes, it took less than three years for Morarji Desai's government to sink. It was helped on its way by Sanjay Gandhi's skilful manipulation of its internal rivalries. Khushwant Singh, the Sikh journalist and historian, was a close friend of Sanjay's at the time and a major architect of the comeback he was planning. He remembers giving a series of intimate dinner parties at his home, where Mrs Gandhi informally met members of the press corps and successfully charmed away their memories of emergency censorship. He also recalls a less savoury episode in which obscene photographs of Jagjivan Ram's son, *in flagrante delicto* with a woman not his wife, proved an effective weapon in neutralising the Janata government's most effective member. The photographs fell into the hands of Sanjay's wife, Maneka, who threatened to publish them in a glossy magazine she edited called *Surya*. Khushwant Singh says he was asked to intercede with Mrs Gandhi to stop her daughter-in-law using the photographs. 'She was thoroughly enjoying that scene,' he chuckles. 'I thought she was a very prudish lady who would be horrified at the use of these pictures with sexual acts of all kinds. But not at all! She said I am not going to stop Maneka from publishing them.'

Tired of Janata's political in-fighting, India put its faith once again in the Nehru–Gandhi dynasty in the general election of January 1980. Sanjay masterminded the campaign and selected the candidates. Mrs Gandhi seemed totally under his influence, says Khushwant Singh, a member of the intimate family circle at that time.

He was a very powerful character, a bit of a bully. She couldn't say 'no' to the man. I wasn't quite able to understand why. She professed a lot of affection for him, but I think in fact she was a little scared of him. I have a feeling that he had some kind of access to family secrets which may have given him some kind of power of blackmail. I don't know. But I felt that, although he was extremely courteous and polite to her – they kept up a lot of formality in this family – there was no stopping him. When he wanted something, he got it done, even if she didn't seem to agree with him.

There was even speculation that Sanjay might oust his mother; but that was not to be. Shortly after the elections, he died, flying his own light aeroplane. As impatient of the rules of flying as he was of political constraints, he crashed performing aerobatics within one mile of the house where he had lived with his mother in the centre of official New Delhi. In life and in death, Sanjay got a bad press. But Dinesh Singh, a veteran of Congress politics, says he had his good points.

He had a style which was very brusque, and he did not have too much time to spend on people talking. He was very precise; and therefore he gave the impression that he was rude. But he had a very large team of different sets of people; and he had a very good channel of information coming to him, and also a good team to execute his orders. To that extent, he appeared ruthless; and he *was* ruthless with opposition. But I don't think that he was devilish in any way.

Indeed, Dinesh Singh seems to have found Sanjay easier to deal with than his imperious mother. 'He was very polite to me,' he recalls. 'He was very considerate. He came to me from time to time for advice, and he supported me. In fact, it was he who brought me back into the party.'

As against such admirers, there were many who heaved a sigh of relief at Sanjay's removal from the political scene, arguing that he would have turned India fascist had he lived. One of them was Romesh Thapar, who broke with Mrs Gandhi over Sanjay's role.

He had evolved a model of political activity which was

quite simple. He said that lots of young men and women with talent were unemployed, and he wanted funds to employ them as activists of the Congress. His ambition was to collect one crore[1] of rupees every day, and he said: 'Nobody will be able to compete with me then.' I think he came very close to it, actually – all those meetings that were organised and the dress-rehearsals for setting up activist brigades of the Congress. The 'fascisation' of the Congress was well under way. After the 1980 election, when Mrs Gandhi came back after the Janata débâcle, Sanjay would have proceeded with it if this accident hadn't cut him off.

Such considerations, of course, did not weigh with a bereaved mother; and Khushwant Singh describes how shattered Mrs Gandhi was by Sanjay's death.

She lost her moorings altogether. She became indecisive, she became petty, and she made wrong decisions all the time. I know that she was unable to sleep for several nights. She over-worked, and at times looked very distracted. You could see her looking at you, but her mind was far away.

Despite the cruel blow that fate had dealt her, Mrs Gandhi did not forsake her dynastic plans. She asked her elder son, Rajiv, to join the family business and had little difficulty in getting her party to accept him as the new heir-apparent. Until his brother's death, Rajiv had kept out of politics, pursuing his career as a pilot with India's state-owned domestic airline. He had lived with his Italian wife, Sonia, in the same house as his mother, brother and sister-in-law Maneka. But it had been a far from happy home, as Khushwant Singh, a frequent visitor, recalls.

There were two sections in that family, and they were even physically divided. In one wing lived Rajiv and Sonia; on the other side were Sanjay, Maneka and her innumerable dogs. She had this huge Irish wolf-hound and two or three massive-sized dogs. You really went to visit one or the other; you never saw the two families

1 A crore is an Indian term for 10 million.

together except at lunchtime briefly. It was a depress-
ing household. And I know for certain that Rajiv was
very unhappy with Sanjay, because he was known to
have said: 'You brought this on our heads. This is all
your doing.' So they were barely on talking terms; they
were very formal with each other.

Khushwant Singh remembers Rajiv as an unwilling candidate
for the greatness that was thrust upon him by his
brother's death. 'When I mentioned the subject,' he recalls,
'Mrs Gandhi repeated many times: "Rajiv has no interest in
politics. Sonia threatens to divorce him if he enters politics."
And then he did enter politics.'

A less reluctant political debutante was Sanjay's young
widow, who left the family house to set up her own political
party, named after her husband. To the elder Mrs Gandhi's
horror, the dynasty now had not only a legitimate Crown
Prince, but also a Young Pretender. Khushwant Singh, whose
loyalty was to Maneka Gandhi, soon found himself out of
favour with her mother-in-law.

Mrs Gandhi was in some ways a very small woman.
She had very strong likes and dislikes, and among her
strongest dislikes was Maneka. She made no secret of
it, even when Sanjay was around. She felt that they
didn't belong to the same class. Maneka was, after all,
very brash in her speech. She was very easy with four-
letter words – charming teenage habits. But Mrs
Gandhi took an instant aversion to her and started
being unfair to her, like a typical Indian mother-in-law
would be. As soon as Sanjay died, she felt what little
inhibition she had about being rough with Maneka go.
Thereafter, anyone she thought was a friend of Maneka's was her enemy; it was as simple as that. Maneka
got quite physically sick with all the slights and barbed
remarks. I know that at formal functions – I think even
when Mrs Gandhi entertained Mrs Thatcher once –
Maneka was hardly ever introduced to the guests but
made to sit with the staff, not with family members.
She knew the time was coming, and she prepared to
leave in her own good time. I think she scored over Mrs
Gandhi in that episode without any difficulty.

Whatever the rights and wrongs of the quarrel between the two Mrs Gandhis, it dominated the Indian press for several months and prompted some unflattering historical comparisons with the twilight of the Mughals, when court intrigues and fraternal feuds had dissipated what was left of a dwindling empire. To some observers, it seemed as though this tasteless, public bickering between a brash young woman and her bossy mother-in-law would prove to be the *reductio ad absurdum* of Indian dynasticism. But events were to show that the dynasty could survive both tragedy and farce. B. K. Nehru, a relative of the ruling family, has restricted his own ambitions to the civil service. He offers some clues as to why the Nehru myth has proved so durable in a functioning democracy.

> The image has been built up of the Nehru family being something superior – maybe rightly, maybe wrongly. One of the basic facts is that the Nehru–Gandhis are one of the few groups of people who can go beyond our diversities, beyond religion and caste, and are truly all-Indian. Very few among our political leaders can say that. Partly, this is due to their training and attitude and upbringing; but partly, it is due to the fact that the Kashmiri Pandits – the community to which we belong – really had no home of their own when they came down from Kashmir 250 years ago. They were like nomads: they moved from place to place. So their loyalties are all-India loyalties and not limited to the region from which they come. Similarly, in the matter of religion or caste, the Nehrus especially, but the Kashmiris also a little more than others, are free from these parochial things.

FORTRESS INDIA

On 2 June 1984, in an operation code-named 'Blue Star', the Indian army encircled the Golden Temple complex in Amritsar. This historic Sikh shrine in the Punjab had been fortified by the Sikh extremist leader, Sant Jarnail Singh Bhindranwale, who was demanding an independent Sikh state called Khalistan. For nearly three years, Bhindranwale had been blatantly defying the authority of the Indian government. He had been stirring up communal hatred by preaching that Sikhs were slaves of Hindus, he had infiltrated the police and the administration, and his young followers seemed able to kill and rob at will. Now Indira Gandhi had finally decided to hit back. On 5 June, the army entered the Golden Temple complex and, in the course of a long and bloody night, suffered 332 casualties. Hundreds of civilians died, and the *Akal Takht*, one of the two most sacred shrines in the complex, was pulverised by squash-head shells fired by tanks.

Khushwant Singh, the Sikh journalist and historian, believes that Mrs Gandhi's military advisers had misled her about the scale of the operation.

I know for certain that she was misadvised. She was told that this operation would be over in two hours. The army, with the information at its disposal, gave her to understand that this would be done. At midnight, when the army asked for permission to move tanks into the compound, because the battle was going very badly, she gave that permission reluctantly. I know that when she went to see the complex two or

three days later, she was absolutely horrified by what
had happened, and she broke down.

The news of the destruction was to be far more traumatic for
the Sikhs themselves, as Khushwant Singh explains.

> It was the great breaking point; since then, the Sikhs
> have never been the same people. Whatever has fol-
> lowed – the tragedies that have occurred one after
> another, the assassination of Mrs Gandhi, the mas-
> sacre of Sikhs in the cities of northern India – are all
> connected with that great blunder, Operation Blue
> Star. The rise of terrorism is connected with Blue Star
> and with what they called Operation Woodrose – that
> was after the occupation of the Golden Temple, when
> the army fanned out into the countryside to hunt for
> young Sikhs suspected of being terrorists. The whole
> history of India has changed, almost I'd say like
> the history of the freedom movement changed after
> Jallianwallah Bagh.[1]

Western journalists had often called Mrs Gandhi the 'Empress
of India'. She could indeed be imperious, but underneath an
often haughty exterior there lay a woman who had many
doubts. Girilal Jain, the editor of the *Times of India*, described
himself as the defender of India against the enemies of Indira
Gandhi after her death; but even he feels she should have taken
action against Bhindranwale before he fortified the Golden
Temple.

> Operation Blue Star was without doubt a mistake, but
> it had become an unavoidable mistake. Indira Gandhi
> should have sent in the police much earlier. But Indira
> Gandhi was really nervous. Those who knew her
> would know that she tended to avoid decisions; that,
> contrary to the popular impression, Indira Gandhi was
> essentially an indecisive person. She postponed a de-
> cision as long as she could no longer postpone it.

Girilal Jain also believes that electoral factors influenced

1 The historic colonial massacre, also in Amritsar, when British troops
opened fire on an unarmed Indian crowd in 1919.

Indira Gandhi's decision to send the army into the Golden Temple: 'The general election was approaching at that time. She was concerned that the Congress Party was not in very good shape. She also knew that her own popularity had shrunk, and she felt she couldn't be seen to be weak at that particular moment.'

Inder Gujral is a Punjabi Hindu who had earlier served as Mrs Gandhi's Information Minister, but was opposed to her during the Punjab crisis. He, too, believes that she had electoral motives for not acting earlier, but interprets them differently.

> In the early stages, I was writing to Mrs Gandhi about the Punjab situation, and she was responding to me from time to time. As time passed, I started to feel that Mrs Gandhi deliberately did not want to defuse this crisis, because she was under the impression that this was a situation which she could switch on and off whenever she wanted to. Therefore, she was perhaps calculating and indeed counting on the fact that this could be a very good issue for elections. Certainly, we in the Opposition collectively had come to the conclusion, I think about a year before the crisis took its ultimate, ugly shape, that Mrs Gandhi would not like to defuse it until after the elections.

The Opposition believed that Mrs Gandhi could have negotiated a settlement with the leaders of the Sikh religious party, the Akali Dal, and thereby gained the support she needed to take action against Bhindranwale. Girilal Jain, however, feels that Mrs Gandhi had good reasons for doubting the reliability of the Akali Dal.

> She had become distrustful of the Akali Dal and had convinced herself that their demands had secessionist undertones. She also believed that external forces were behind them and feared that, once their present demands were conceded or negotiated successfully, they would raise other demands. There is a background to this. When Indira Gandhi conceded the Akalis' demand for a separate Punjabi-speaking state

just after she came to power, the Akali leadership assured her this was their last demand. It was not, of course, and so Indira Gandhi, rightly or wrongly, became distrustful of them. She could not overcome this suspicion.

In the event, Operation Blue Star certainly outraged moderate Sikhs and played into the hands of the extremists. Four months later, India paid a tragic price for it when Indira Gandhi was shot by two of her bodyguards, both Sikhs, in the garden of her house in Delhi. The Prime Minister's assassination was a tribute to her undoubted courage. She had been advised not to have any Sikhs in her bodyguard after Operation Blue Star, but she had refused to accept that she could no longer trust members of an Indian community.

Indira Gandhi had towered over India for nineteen years. She was the only national leader, and a much respected international leader too. Throughout her long career she was bitterly criticised by India's querulous élite; but till the end of her life she retained a unique place in the hearts of the Indian people who had flocked to greet her wherever she went. But even they deserted her on her last journey. Fear kept Indira Gandhi's followers away from her funeral cortège as it moved slowly down *Raj Path*, which leads from the presidential palace to the flame of eternal life burning beneath the India Gate war memorial. Fear also kept them away from her last rites, celebrated on the banks of the River Jamuna where her father, Jawaharlal Nehru, and her son, Sanjay, had been cremated.

Anti-Sikh riots broke out in Delhi on the evening of the day Indira Gandhi was assassinated. They were the worst riots India had seen since the holocaust of partition. The police force collapsed, often collaborating openly with the rioters. Two highly reputable civil rights organisations, which conducted enquiries into the riots, maintain that local Congress Party leaders instigated the violence. One of their reports said: 'In the areas which were most affected, the mobs were led by local Congress politicians and hoodlums of those localities.' The riots spread to other parts of northern and eastern India. Only the Communist government in Calcutta tackled them effectively. The official figure of those killed – 2717 – is appalling enough. Unofficial figures are even higher. Almost all the dead were Sikhs, some of them deliberately burnt to death by rioters.

Khushwant Singh describes his own experience of those two days when the centuries-old relationship between his community and the Hindus broke down.

> I got a frantic telephone call from my friends who were monitoring the rioters' movements. They told me [the rioters] were coming for me. I rang up the President's[1] household and told him about the danger. All his secretary could tell me was: 'The President says you had better move to the house of a Hindu.' So I said, in as acid a tone as I could manage: 'If that's all the advice and help the President can give me at this moment, just thank him on my behalf.' I moved to my daughter's house next door – she is married to a Hindu. Then fortunately for me, through the intervention of [journalist] Romesh Thapar, who took a very active part in helping many people, members of the Swedish Embassy came and picked me up. I left my house with just my toothbrush and toothpaste and the manuscript I was working on. For the first time I felt a refugee in my own country.

Khushwant Singh believes that the riots could easily have been controlled.

> I have not the slightest doubt that a few armed jeeps with armed policemen, with orders to shoot at sight, would have seen to it that there was none of this. The goons were deliberately allowed to get together. They were directed by the people of the Congress Party. They gathered people armed with rods and brought them in trucks with gallons of petrol. These people then went about looting shops and killing Sikhs, burning them alive with the police watching. At my own gate on that first night we watched these things going on. The whole city was burning, you could see fires from our roof-tops; we could see the smoke coming up.

1 The President of India, Giani Zail Singh, was a Sikh.

Rajiv Gandhi was mourning his mother and seemed unaware of the scale of the violence which had engulfed his capital. It was only after he went out very early on the third morning of the riots to see for himself that he took decisive action and called on the army to end the mayhem. Khushwant Singh explains Rajiv's failure to take action.

> I give him the benefit of the doubt. He had suffered the terrible tragedy of his mother's assassination, and he was not able to react properly. But I think there was a criminal waste of time during those two days when Rajiv stood by his mother's body receiving VIPs from foreign countries, while the city was going up in flames. All he needed to do was to come out then and say this must stop. Apparently the President made several requests that the army should be brought in, and it was not. When the army did eventually come in, it didn't really start acting until the third day. By then five thousand people or more had been murdered.

It is evidence of the durability of the Nehru dynasty that hardly a second thought was given to the succession when Indira Gandhi was assassinated. By precedent, the most senior member of the government should have been sworn in as interim Prime Minister, until the Congress members of parliament could meet to elect a new leader. Rajiv Gandhi had only been in active politics for four years and held no office in his mother's government. Nevertheless the President swore him in on the day Indira Gandhi died, and the Congress members of parliament automatically endorsed that decision. He was the youngest and most inexperienced Prime Minister that India had ever known. Until the death of his brother Sanjay in 1980, he had appeared content to pursue his career as an airline pilot. Even when Sanjay died, Rajiv was reluctant to come into politics as his great-aunt, Vijayalakshmi Pandit, recalls.

> Rajiv wasn't very close to his mother, while Sanjay and she were very close to each other. I remember very well when Sanjay died, we were all waiting for Rajiv at two o'clock in the morning when he came back from Italy.

When he came in, a lot of people rushed at him – I thought it was very bad manners. They said: 'You must stand by your mother,' not giving him a chance to think for himself. He said to me: 'I'm very happy as I am in my profession, and I don't know enough about politics, so what help can I give her?' I believe that was based on something she said just before he left for his holiday in Italy. Sanjay was saying something which Rajiv contradicted, and she said: 'Oh, please don't contradict. You don't know politics.'

Nevertheless, Mrs Pandit believes that her great-nephew has the ability to rule India: 'Of course, at the moment he has his hands full of trouble, but I think he is a very fine person. I believe he has it in him to rise and be straight and do what people think he ought to do.'

When Rajiv Gandhi first came to power, he spoke of bringing India into the twenty-first century. He wanted to unscramble the ramshackle bureaucracy, to liberate the economy, and to free Indians to exploit their undoubted talents as traders and industrialists. To help him, he brought in modern young men, mostly with westernised education and ideas.

Girilal Jain of the *Times of India* does not approve of the new-style politicians.

These safari-suited young men are far more arrogant than their predecessors, but that is not the heart of my concern. The heart of my concern is that these young men are far less able to relate themselves to the society they represent. Their predecessors were a kind of bridge between the people of India and the Western-educated, or at least English-language-educated, bureaucracy. The new young men will be less able to play this mediatory role, and that is a very major criticism.

It would appear that Rajiv Gandhi agrees with the editor of the *Times of India*, because he has come to depend much more on the old school of Congressmen who prefer Indian dress; but much of the reforming zeal of the government appears to have gone out with the safari-suit brigade. Even so, L. K. Jha, who has now been economic adviser to three generations of the Nehru family, says that Rajiv Gandhi is much more committed to reform than his mother.

> Take the business of economic reforms. Although I know that personally she was in favour of most of the recommendations which I made, she would let the ministries and departments handle them. The fate of those recommendations, therefore, depended very much on how the ministers and the bureaucracy responded to them. Rajiv is excited about economic reforms, so he is putting himself behind them, which his mother was not prepared to do.

During his first year in office it seemed as though Rajiv Gandhi could do no wrong. Even the Opposition found little to criticise. But Ramakrishna Hegde, seen by many as the Opposition's best candidate for the prime ministership, suggests that Rajiv's early successes went to his head.

> He started his career as Prime Minister on a note of great promise. He wanted to remove corruption; he wanted to bring back decent traditions; he wanted, above all, to hold elections within his own party; and he wanted to keep a continuous dialogue with various Opposition leaders going on various national issues. But one after another, all these promises seem to have been forgotten. I think the adulation that he received in the early stages has made him arrogant. He started with such a tremendous fund of goodwill. His behaviour with both the Opposition and the bureaucracy was very conscientious; you could hardly point out any mistakes. Now he appears to take most of these things very lightly. There isn't enough seriousness about him, and he doesn't appear to think before he speaks.

One victim of Rajiv Gandhi's tendency to shoot from the hip is A. P. Venkateswaran. He learnt that Rajiv Gandhi was thinking of sacking him as Foreign Secretary[1] from a chance remark

1 The senior civil servant in the External Affairs Ministry.

the Prime Minister made at a news conference. Venkateswaran ended his long and distinguished diplomatic career that
day by resigning. He believes that it is wrong for politicians
like Rajiv Gandhi to blame the bureaucrats for the government's mistakes.

> The job of the bureaucratic elements in the Foreign
> Office is to collect facts, analyse them, interpret them,
> and to put certain options before the political lead-
> ership. It is then for the political leadership to choose
> one or other of the options, or a combination of them.
> So whenever there is a failure in foreign policy, as they
> keep saying, it has nothing to do with the civil servants
> and everything to do with the politicians. When all is
> said and done, bureaucracy is only an instrument in
> the hands of the political leadership, and it's a bad
> workman who blames his tools.

One of Rajiv Gandhi's greatest assets when he first came to
power was his reputation for incorruptibility. The Indian press
called him 'Mr Clean' and took his promises to eradicate
corruption seriously. Then came a series of alleged scandals
involving his government, and V. P. Singh, the minister head-
ing his anti-corruption drive, resigned, on the grounds that the
government was not investigating these allegations seriously.
Singh is a much respected figure; and when he failed to get a
hearing in the Congress Party, he joined the Opposition and
raised the banner of revolt. In spite of the furore whipped up
by the Opposition, nothing has been proved against Rajiv
Gandhi or anyone close to him; but the press no longer calls
him Mr Clean.

Rajiv Gandhi has also earned himself a reputation for
being inaccessible. His mother made a point of meeting as
many people as she could. She was always particularly careful
to be available to members of her party. Rajiv Gandhi has all
the charm of the Nehru family, but his opportunities for
turning on that charm are restricted by the tight security
surrounding him because of the threat from Sikh extremists.
The special commando force he has raised, known as the
'Black Cats', have turned his house into a fortress and his
family into prisoners. His children's teachers have to come to

them, since they cannot go to school; and Rajiv himself teaches his son computer science. Then again, Rajiv Gandhi is the first Indian prime minister to have a young family. He, his Italian wife Sonia, and their two children are a very closely knit family; and this puts demands on Rajiv Gandhi's time which no other Indian prime minister has faced.

Inevitably, Rajiv Gandhi has also come up against powerful vested interests. His early successes caused a backlash from the very people threatened by his reforming zeal – the politicians and bureaucrats who made money out of the economic controls and the shortages he was trying to remove. He backed down on some of his economic measures when his party told him they went against its socialist tradition. He backed down on the sensible accord he had signed to end the confrontation with the Sikh religious party in the Punjab when his party told him it was damaging its electoral prospects in the crucial Hindi-speaking states of north India.

Rajiv Gandhi was not entirely to blame. His mother had not exactly encouraged talent in the Congress Party, so there was no base on which to build support for his new policies. Girilal Jain points out that the rot in the Congress Party started long before Indira Gandhi.

> The degeneration of the Congress Party began immediately after independence. When Jawaharlal Nehru was very much alive and at the height of his power, the Gandhi-cap[1] came to symbolise corruption. The Congress Party was in very bad shape by the time that Indira Gandhi came to power. The valid criticism against Indira Gandhi would be that she made no earnest effort to rehabilitate the Congress Party. For one thing, she was not terribly interested in the Congress Party; she did not have much respect for it. The task of rehabilitating Congress was also immensely difficult, as you can see from the failure of Rajiv Gandhi to hold elections to the party organisation.

During her last term in office, Indira Gandhi used to warn the

[1] The white cap, made of *khadi* or homespun cloth, which was the uniform of a Congressman during the independence struggle and in the early days of independence. Jawaharlal Nehru wore one throughout his prime ministership.

political meetings she addressed that the unity of India was being threatened. This was also Rajiv Gandhi's theme in the highly successful election campaign he fought to confirm his prime ministership after his mother's death. Was it, and indeed is it, just a political slogan to persuade voters to rally behind the family which has held India together for so long; or is there really a threat to the unity of the world's largest democracy?

The Congress Party remains the only truly national party, a party which is at least an important force in every state of India. The main challenge to it comes from regional parties, strong in their own states, but with little or no presence outside them. It is not surprising, therefore, that Rajiv Gandhi and the Congress Party identify the growing regionalism in India as a major threat to the nation's unity. Regionalism in its most extreme form, like the Khalistan movement for Sikh independence, is a threat to the unity of India. Regionalism in its constitutional form – the demand for more powers for state governments – is probably not a threat.

It is in southern India that the Congress Party has suffered worst at the hands of regional parties. Ramakrishna Hegde, the Chief Minister of the southern state of Karnataka, explains why he believes it is in India's interest to accept his party's demand to give greater autonomy to state governments.

> Even though our constitution is essentially federal, several unitary features have been introduced. I think this is partly because of the peculiar situation at the time of independence, partly because of the dominance of one single personality, and partly because one single party has ruled the whole country. Certain powers that belong to the state governments were surrendered to the central government. In practice, even though the constitution does not provide for it, the central government assumed greater powers. This has created a lot of frustration, and I'm quite sure that one remedy for the growing feeling of regional identity is to give greater autonomy to the states.

The distinguished constitutional lawyer L. M. Singhvi believes that the problem goes even deeper than the state level. 'The state governments,' he says, 'will have to learn to allow more

power to be devolved to the institutions of local self-govern-
ment in order to make our democracy really successful and
effective. This grass-roots democracy cannot be denied for too
long.'

The argument against this point of view is that local bodies
are entirely dominated by the more prosperous farmers, traders and bureaucrats and that they would grab the power and
the resources devolved by the state governments. Dr Singhvi
has an answer to that.

> There is a danger of grass-roots democracy getting
> bogged down in a struggle for resources; but in spite of
> that, I think democracy has to work itself out through
> a democratic process, through creating a culture of
> democracy. I don't think that the people of India
> would tolerate for long the distortion of the demo-
> cratic process, if only they had the opportunity to do
> something about it at the grass-roots level. I would
> trust the common man much more than the politician;
> and it is the common man who can, in the long run,
> discipline the politician.

Another political threat to the unity of India which is much
talked about is the growing aggressiveness of north Indian
Hindus. Professor Rajni Kothari, an internationally renowned
political scientist, explains the reasons for their mounting
anger.

> The feeling is that the majority community has suf-
> fered, that somehow because of the tremendous liber-
> alism of the Indian nation, the Sikhs and the Muslims,
> who are the minorities, have done better economically
> and are still given greater opportunities. Again the
> Hindus feel that the Tribals and the Untouchables are
> given all sorts of reserved opportunities, and here are
> we, the large majority community, left at a loose end. I
> have even heard leaders, both in the government and in
> parties like the Bhartiya Janata Party, which is a Hindu
> party, saying that what the Hindus lack is a central
> church, a monastic order, a kind of clergy, like the
> Christians and the Muslims. Ironically the power of

the Hindu myth, the strength of the Hindu identity, was precisely that it did not need churches, monastic orders and clergy. What kept the Hindu identity alive was the fact that there was no one Hindu.

For many years the Congress Party and the ruling dynasty kept the more strident elements among the north Indian Hindus in check. It insisted that the majority should not be allowed to dominate the country, that the voice of the minorities should be heard too. Professor Kothari believes this is no longer so.

Nehru's approach, and the approach of Mrs Gandhi in her early days, was to appeal more to the poor, the minorities and the south. As Mrs Gandhi began to suffer electoral losses, she withdrew into this sort of north Indian, Hindu identity. What you are now getting is a kind of crystallisation of Indian nationalism into north India, a kind of Fortress-Hindu-India in north India. It will not only be the undoing of the minorities; it will be the undoing of the country.

The threat to India's unity that Rajiv Gandhi speaks most of is 'the foreign hand'. The hand is also the symbol of the Congress Party. Cartoonists have inevitably drawn the Congress Party symbol and asked: 'Is this the hand which is really threatening India?' Traditionally the main danger has been seen as coming from Pakistan. According to Girilal Jain, it is the China–Pakistan axis which has worried India most.

India has been apprehensive for a long time, certainly since the mid-sixties, that China looks upon Pakistan as a proxy for creating problems in India. China wants to deny us what we regard as our legitimate place in the sub-Himalayan region at least, if not in the larger region which could include the Gulf. As I see it, and as I think Indira Gandhi saw it, the problem with China is not mainly the border dispute, it's China's perception of India's role in South Asia.

Since he came to power, Rajiv Gandhi has been stressing the danger from the US–Pakistan axis. The United States has been re-arming Pakistan, and Rajiv Gandhi believes this is a serious threat to India. He has also been warning the world that Pakistan is building the bomb. Although Pakistan vigorously denies it is going nuclear, even the United States takes this threat seriously. But there are those in India who believe that a nuclear sub-continent would be in the country's interest. There is no doubt that India, with its sophisticated nuclear power industry, its research laboratories, and its space programmes, could build its own bomb. The leading protagonist of the nuclear lobby in India is K. Subrahmanyam of the Institute of Defence Studies and Analysis in Delhi. He is most emphatic that going nuclear is the best way to halt India's spiralling defence costs.

> The question of our defence is inherent in our geography. We are surrounded by three major nuclear arsenals: the Soviet Union, China, and America on the high seas. We are also garlanded by smaller states, all of which have to struggle for an independent identity vis-à-vis India. So under those circumstances the present defence budget is inescapable. Now, if we were to go nuclear, we would be able to cap the rise in defence expenditure. If India does not go nuclear, the sense of insecurity here will push our defence expenditure through the roof.

Subrahmanyam does not believe that there is a danger of a nuclear war if India and Pakistan both get the bomb.

> Take the European experience. You people have been fighting for three hundred years. Just count the number of wars that you fought in Europe and count the fact that you fought two world wars within thirty years in the first half of this century. Now there is peace in Europe, and many people, including Mrs Thatcher, feel very insecure without nuclear weapons.

The super-powers and Europe have put tremendous pressure on both India and Pakistan to prevent them joining the nuclear club. Indira Gandhi did resist this pressure in 1974 when she exploded what she called a 'peaceful' nuclear device; but she never repeated the experiment. Subrahmanyam resents the international pressure on India.

> I think it's a carry-over of the White Man's Burden. It's a carry-over of the nineteenth century, when the European-centred comity of nations felt they had to rule the rest of the world; the Nuclear Non-Proliferation Treaty is a continuation of that. It is nuclear colonialism.

Subrahmanyam angrily rejects the argument that nuclear weapons would be less safe in the hands of India and Pakistan than in the hands of the present members of the club.

> As the Israelis took their enriched uranium from the United States, it's quite obvious things are not safe in America. We know very well that the Pakistanis obtained all their equipment from Western European countries and from the United States. When somebody is caught red-handed smuggling krypton switches to Pakistan, the American courts let him off with a nominal sentence. So do the Canadians. I would like to know how safe things are in their part of the world and what makes them think it will be worse in our part of the world.

Does India have its own colonial ambitions? Is it India which is destabilising South Asia? Some of its smaller neighbours have their doubts. Without Mrs Gandhi's intervention there would have been no Bangladesh. Now Rajiv Gandhi's troops are fighting Tamil extremists in Sri Lanka, admittedly at the request of the Sri Lankan government. These interventions may produce short-term gains for India, but in the long run they heighten the smaller South Asian countries' fears of their huge neighbour. The former Foreign Secretary, A. P. Venkateswaran, believes that India's all too brief honeymoon with Bangladesh shows that its relations with its neighbours will always be delicate.

> Sure enough there was a honeymoon period. That was only to be expected, because we had shed Indian blood

to help the people of Bangladesh liberate themselves. But you must remember that any large country with small countries on its periphery has difficulties in having honeymoons. This is true of China, of the United States, of the Soviet Union, and for that matter of India. We have to learn to live with it and to show the patience, tolerance and understanding to manage our relationships with our smaller neighbours without expecting honeymoons.

If India does not handle relations with its neighbours sensitively, the great powers will get involved, and that really will be a threat to the nation's unity. That threat could well be brought on by the aggressive Fortress India attitude that Professor Kothari warned about.

GIVING AND TAKING

When the British left India in 1947, they left behind them a backward, poverty-stricken, agricultural nation with a small, colonial-style ruling élite. The historian, Bipin Chandra, has written: 'All the euphoria of freedom in 1947 could not hide the ugly reality of the colonial legacy that India inherited – the misery, the mud and filth. In the economic sphere, as in others, British rule had drastically transformed India. However, the changes that had come had led only to the development of under-development.' Chandra described the results of colonialisation as 'the pauperisation of the people, especially the peasantry, and the presence of extreme and visible poverty and starvation.'

In many ways, India has made tremendous progress since independence, and is now a major industrial power with a vast, new middle class. Between 1950 and 1984, for example, the annual production of steel increased from 1.04 million to 6.90 million tonnes. In the same period, cement production went up from 2.70 million to 29.90 million tonnes and the production of coal from 32.80 million to 155.20 million tonnes. The average life expectancy of the people has gone up, too – from 32 years in 1947 to 57 years now.

Of course India is still very far from being a land flowing with milk and honey. Famine no longer stalks the land, but millions of Indians are still poverty-stricken and backward. Even in their case, a great change has taken place. Forty years of democracy have taught even the poorest of the poor that they do have rights, says Ela Bhatt, who founded a voluntary organisation to help working-class women.

Wherever I travel I find that men and women also are getting more and more aware about their own condition, which is very bad, and about their rights. Through the media, through newspapers, and through word of mouth, they also know about the various services and schemes which are available to them. When the government or the others are not able to reach them, this creates a sort of frustration, because they have these high expectations.

This frustration is all the greater when, as happens all too often, people find that they have to pay for government services which should be free. There was, for instance, a young man running a small tea-stall near the town of Jamunanagar in north India. He approached a branch of a nationalised bank with an approved application for a loan to buy a cow. The manager of the bank said to him: 'You can have the loan if you pay me my percentage.' The man replied: 'Then I won't be able to buy the cow because I won't have enough money.' To which the bank manager replied: 'Well you can't buy one anyhow, can you?'

The journalist and economist, Prem Shankar Jha, warns that there could be anarchy if the rising expectations of Indians are not met.

In the final analysis, slow growth means slow growth of employment. Slow growth of employment means growing unrest and one of two things will happen. The representatives of the classes who have a stake in India's protected and controlled economic system will perceive the danger that is coming and change. This is what is happening to some extent already – slowly, but it is happening. The massive liberalisations which Rajiv Gandhi has put through are not without support from industrialists, and particularly large industrialists. But if that doesn't happen, or doesn't happen fast enough, you will get either a revolution or, more likely in the Indian circumstances, a general collapse into anarchy. Long before that happens, the oppressive machinery of the government will have to be strengthened, and strengthened, and strengthened. This is what I think is actually happening just now in India.

The police and the paramilitary forces are being expanded and given more modern equipment, but violence seems to be expanding too. 1987 saw continuing Sikh terrorism in Punjab, violent strikes by Nepalis demanding their own state in the Darjeeling hills, massacres in the caste-war in Bihar, and Hindu–Muslim clashes in northern India. In any other Third World country, such violence would lead to fears of a military coup, yet somehow in India no one seems to believe in such a possibility. One reason is the army itself. It is still a very traditional army, and that sort of army does not usually get involved in coups.

General Vohra, a former Vice-Chief of the Army Staff, explains the importance of tradition in the Indian Army.

> Tradition has been defined by Field Marshal Slim as not handing down a lower standard of courage, conduct and duty than was given to you. Now this tradition is based on a large number of things. Ceremonial is a big part of it. Ceremonial is normally spit-and-polish-and-bull. But it motivates the soldier, it gives him *esprit de corps*, it gives him the ability to sacrifice himself for the honour of the regiment. Tradition is built up on all these bits and pieces, whether it is uniforms, or badges, or a particular ceremonial like the handing of a guidon or a flag or colours to a regiment. These things have been done in this army in some regiments for almost two hundred years; therefore the ethos of the regiment is tied up with all these rituals and ceremonials. Then there is the human connection, whether it was the British officers who served in the same regiments for generations, or now in our case many of us who have served in the same regiment for two or three generations. I think some of these things will carry on for ever. No regiment will give up any of its ceremonial or its associations of which it is proud.

It is not just tradition which has kept the Indian army out of politics. In Pakistan, the army inherited the same traditions but has played a major role in politics. General Vohra thinks the institutions of India have saved the army.

I think we were lucky, in that Nehru in the early years established and institutionalised our body politic. He defined the roles of the various elements – the legislature, the judiciary and so on. The armed forces are also an element. Their primary task is the defence of the country. Because of that institutionalisation, the army has been quite content with its task of defence and has had no political ambitions. In Pakistan, the institutionalisation either did not take place or did not gel, and the armed forces found themselves in circumstances where they had to step in.

India does have all the institutions needed to preserve democracy. It has elected politicians to make policy. It has a bureaucracy to implement those policies. It has a free press to act as a watchdog on the politicians and the bureaucrats. It has courts to try and, if necessary, punish those who break the law. It has a Supreme Court to make sure that laws passed by the politicians do not violate the fundamental principles of the constitution. But how healthy are these institutions?

Parliament is the centre of India's democracy. Like the British House of Commons, India's *Lok Sabha*, or House of the People, can be a noisy and chaotic affair. While the older generation feels that parliamentary standards are slipping, many Indian MPs feel that the role of Parliament itself is being undermined, that the government does not treat the House with the respect which is its due. The central government and state governments do frequently bypass the legislatures by introducing ordinances. Bihar, which is traditionally a Congress state, is one of the worst offenders. Between 1971 and 1981, successive Bihar governments passed 163 acts. The total number of ordinances promulgated was 287. As Nilankantha Rath, Director of the Institute of Politics and Economics, has said: 'The failure of the legislature is an alarming development for the democratic polity of India.'

Many senior bureaucrats think that the administration has gone down too. One of them is R. D. Pradhan, who recently retired as Home Secretary.

Problems arising out of the population explosion, educated unemployment, unplanned urban growth, scarcity of resources, degradation of ecology, are innumerable and pose stupendous challenges to any administration. The experience of our administrative structure for the past four decades does not encourage the belief that we are equipped to tackle these and the many other problems that the country will face. Unless corrective action is taken at this stage, there is a real danger of the collapse of the administrative structure, and perhaps of the democratic framework.

The constitutional lawyer, Dr Singhvi, is equally concerned about the state of the courts.

The courts are almost at breaking point because of arrears and delays. This is not something which arose suddenly, only yesterday. We have been talking about it for the last thirty years; we have been talking of reform but doing too little and too late. I think there is not a clear enough political will in the matter, partly because citizens are not enlightened and vigilant enough. I don't see why our legal system cannot be restructured and recast. Parliament must find the time; the judiciary must find the time; the executive must find the time.

A leading opposition politician, V. P. Singh, who was once Chief Minister of Uttar Pradesh, India's most populous state, has this to say about the administration of justice in India: 'Those above the poverty line are above the gaol line. Those whose coffers are full will not go to prison.'

India and Indians pay a heavy price for their ineffectual courts. In 1980, a crime wave was sweeping through the previously unremarkable town of Bhagalpur in the state of Bihar. The police were smarting under the taunts of the local press and the public. No sooner did they arrest a suspected criminal, than he managed to get bail from the courts. So the police decided to teach the criminals a lesson. Among those caught in their dragnet was Baljit Singh, the son of a fruit-seller. Baljit was thrown into a jeep and driven to the police station. He was ordered to lie down in the bottom of a lorry. Policemen held him down, forced his eyes open and pierced them with a bicycle spoke. Then a man in a white shirt, referred to by the police as 'Doctor Sahib', injected acid into his eyes. He was taken back to a cell and locked up with six other blinded prisoners. Among them was Saligram Shah, the son of a goldsmith. Shah says that he was taken before the same 'Doctor Sahib' twice. The second time, he was asked whether he could still see anything. When he replied: 'a little', the 'Doctor Sahib' injected his eyes again. The so-called doctor was the last man that Saligram Shah ever saw. Both men still protest that they had committed no crime; and at least twenty-six people were blinded by the police before this barbarity was ended. Even then, the police were not exactly repentant. A senior police official in the state capital of Patna said: 'The police resort to atrocities while dealing with criminals because they do not find the traditional methods of justice effective. There has been a near-total collapse of criminal justice; trials are pending in courts for years. Police find themselves caught in a cycle of crime which they do not know how to break without resorting to third-degree methods.'

Mrs Gandhi has often been accused of deliberately destroying the institutions of India because they stood in the way of her exercising absolute power. In fact, she only took deliberate action against these institutions during the Emergency, but even her admirer, Girilal Jain, admits that she did not exactly cherish them.

> To say that Indira Gandhi destroyed the institutions of India would be to put the criticism rather harshly. If you were to say that she was not sufficiently sensitive to the need for strong institutions in the country, I would go along with you. I would regard the manner in which she treated the bureaucracy as really the most serious criticism of Indira Gandhi. Here was an institution which could have served her purpose and enabled her to vest as much power in her own hands as she deemed necessary, and yet served the larger purposes of India. By demoralising the bureaucracy, she neither served her own interests nor the interests of the country.

Rajiv Gandhi has instituted some reforms of the civil service and modernised some aspects of the training of bureaucrats. His Act preventing politicians defecting from their parties at will has also introduced welcome stability in state governments. There is, however, still no sign of the major overhaul of the bureaucracy and the other institutions which many Indians see as essential if democracy is to survive. Nevertheless, General Vohra does not accept the widely held view that Indian institutions are in danger of collapsing.

> I would not say that the institutions are working well. They have always had shortfalls and that is because of certain feudal trends which still continue in our society. After all India has not had experience of running a country since the sixteenth century. Most institutions the world over developed in the eighteenth and nineteenth centuries. We have only had about forty years experience of running these institutions; and, with the backdrop of this feudalistic background we have, it will take us some time to improve the institutions. The institutions are not satisfactory but I think there are chances of their getting better.

Perhaps General Vohra is right; and perhaps we all expect too much of India's young democracy. For all its faults, it is still upholding the values of a free society against odds not faced in any other democratic country. Indian democracy also has some unusual successes to its credit. For instance, it has democratised Communism. The world's first democratically elected Communist government came to power in the Indian state of Kerala; and in West Bengal, the Communists have been in power for the last ten years. Somnath Chatterjee, a Communist MP from West Bengal, says his party is 'absolutely committed' to democracy.

> Through parliamentary means we have not only been able to form governments in three states, but we are also becoming more and more powerful; more and more people are coming to us. In the parliamentary system, it is only the Communist Party which can project itself as the alternative. People are becoming

more and more conscious that the present dynastic system of government has hopelessly failed.

But Somnath Chatterjee thinks it will be some time before we see a Communist government in parliament in Delhi. The Communist movement shows the same fissiparous tendencies as other Indian political parties. There is the Communist Party of India, which is tied to Moscow, and the more independent and electorally more successful Communist Party (Marxist). There are also countless splinter groups of the Marxist–Leninist movement who, for the most part, advocate violence.

The Communist movement has also been affected by the regionalism, or perhaps one should say parochialism, of India. For instance the Communist Party (Marxist), which is in power in Bengal, is regarded as nothing more than a Bengali party in other parts of eastern India. But this very parochialism can sometimes be one of India's greatest strengths. The plight of the Sri Lankan Tamils is an issue in the Indian state of Tamil Nadu, but of no concern to neighbouring Keralites. Biharis take little or no interest in the battle for a separate Nepali state, taking place in neighbouring West Bengal. Since the independence movement, there has never been a nationwide movement which has threatened the unity or the stability of India, although there have been many violent agitations which have temporarily destabilised parts of the country.

Another striking feature of Indian democracy is its capacity for self-criticism. A stranger reading the daily newspapers would think that no one was honest, no one was efficient, no one was hard-working. Their editorials paint a dismal picture of Indian democracy. But not all Indians are Jeremiahs. The historian Ravindra Kumar of the Nehru Memorial Museum believes that during the last forty years India has built up the infrastructure of a comparatively prosperous society. The task he feels now is to build on the foundations already laid.

Forty years from independence, we are facing what I would call second-generation problems. Take the problem of the economy and the ownership of land in our country. In the fifties, the major problem for the state was to mediate between peasants and feudal lords. I think that today the major problem the state

faces is to mediate between small landlords and peasants, on the one hand, and sharecroppers, tenants and
agricultural labourers, on the other. The whole debate
has been transferred to an altogether different plane.
Then again, if you look at industry, something like a
powerful national grid of skills and economic activity
has been created. What is on the agenda now is to push
down this national grid to our district towns and sub-
district towns, to develop agro-industry, and the
engineering skills which are appropriate to small-scale
entrepreneurship.

India's economic development has produced powerful groups
with a vested interest in the nation's unity. There are the
businessmen and industrialists, the bureaucrats, and indeed
the armed forces. Nevertheless there are still prophets of
gloom who forecast that India will break up under the strain of
competing demands for scarce resources and the population
explosion. They point to the diversity of India, its different
ethnic groups, its castes, its creeds and its many different
languages. India's regions do have their own rich and varied
cultural traditions, but running through them are certain
strong common strands. One of them is Hinduism and its two
great epics, which remain a major source of artistic
inspiration.

There has been a striking renaissance of Indian classical
culture since independence. When we went to the cultural
centre at Kalakshetra in the southern city of Madras, we found
students rehearsing a ballet based on one of the two great
Hindu epics, the *Ramayana*. They were rehearsing in a theatre
which has been built in traditional style, naturally cooled by
sea breezes. Other students were studying classical music and
dance in a cluster of thatched huts surrounding a magnificent,
old banyan tree. The huts were small, emphasising that individual tuition, based on the ancient tradition of the *guru* and
shishya or disciple, is the teaching method at Kalakshetra.
S. Rajaram, the Principal of the College of Fine Arts at
Kalakshetra, told us that the College was dedicated to teaching
and producing only classical dance and music, but he maintained that this did not affect its popularity.

There is plenty of demand for our students and for our performances. There are so many schools now where our students go as teachers. I don't think there is any household in the south, perhaps even in the north, where somebody or other is not learning *Bharata Natyam*.[1] It is so popular. The cultural renaissance is reaching all the people, even the lower middle classes. In this institute particularly, we have kept the fees reasonable, so that even lower middle-class people who are interested in us can come and study here. There is also a terrible demand for tickets when we produce a new production. We keep the price as low as possible, so that people can come and see the production.

The government-controlled All India Radio has produced an artistic hybrid by harmonising Indian music, which by tradition is purely melodic. Rajaram does not approve of this: 'The question is, do they respect music and understand how to popularise it? Personally, I feel West should be West, and East should be East. But I have to admit some people do like it.'

South India has also been a bastion of classical purity because it was not greatly influenced by the Muslim invaders from the north. The Muslims made north Indian culture more eclectic, as we found when we visited the centre for teaching *Kathak* dancing in Delhi. *Kathak* has echoes of the Middle East and even gypsy flamenco. We found Rewa Vidyarthi, one of India's most famous dance teachers, holding a class for young beginners. She was telling them that learning *Kathak* was like learning a language and there were no short cuts. It was certainly much more energetic than learning any language we had ever tried to master.

Delhi has also become a centre of theatre. Kavita Nagpal, an actress, director and arts journalist, took us to the National School of Drama. She explained to us that, during the British Raj, classical culture declined because there was little or no government patronage, and both dance and theatre became associated with prostitution.

1 The most classical and austere of Indian dance forms.

I come from Kanpur where we had a strong tradition of folk theatre called *Nautanki*. I remember in my childhood there was no theatre, because *Nautanki* had fallen on bad days. It had become almost a platform for prostitution, and so it had been banned from the municipal limits of Kanpur. If we wanted to see *Nautanki* we had to go outside Kanpur.

Kavita Nagpal believes that, even today, if you want to see Indian theatre in its natural surroundings, you still have to go outside the cities. 'If you go into the villages,' she says, 'you will find there that people will come in their hundreds and thousands to see traditional theatre because it is part of their lives; it emerges from their roots; it is part of their cultural ethos, their everyday existence. In the urban areas, theatre is more or less superimposed on the lives of people.'

At the National School of Drama, we watched a rehearsal of a musical play by Rabindranath Tagore, the Bengali Nobel prize-winner who pioneered modern Indian theatre at the turn of the century. Young men wearing bright blue trousers, with red cross-belts strapped across their bare chests and loosely tied grey turbans, were practising martial arts. The director, Rita Ganguli, Associate Professor of Mime and Movement, explained what was going on.

These young men are all grown-ups who have joined us as national scholars, and so they have to be given training in body-discipline, as well as our traditional skills like mime – we have a rich tradition of mime. We have chosen this particular play because it is an early one. When Tagore became more mature, he gave a lot of instructions. But this play does not have so many do's and don'ts, and it's a very loosely woven plot, so that the students can improvise a lot, which is the main aim of the class.

The students of the National School of Drama are by no means all from privileged backgrounds. We watched the daughter of a driver rehearsing a Eugene O'Neill play translated into Hindi. O'Neill might seem to be rather far removed from the concerns of an Indian villager; but Kavita Nagpal insisted that the students we watched would not just join the cultural ghettos of the big cities of India. 'After they have finished their training,' she assured us, 'at least fifty per cent of the students will go back to the regions they have come from. They will make use of their training and their learning and do theatre there. Some, of course, will go into films or theatre, but the more serious students will go back to their regions.'

Independent India has produced its own modern pop culture, too. It is based on the film industry, the largest in the world, and Bombay is India's Hollywood. To be a star is a passport to wealth and fame and sometimes to political power. The Chief Ministers of two Indian states have been film stars who founded their political careers on the support of their fans. But India also has a serious cinema, and some stars have managed to straddle the two. One of them was Smita Patil, equally at home in a rain-drenched sari as the heroine of a Bombay blockbuster and as a pavement-dweller in a new-wave film about the slums of Bombay. She died very young. Just before her death she explained why films have such an impact in India.

> The major audience for a normal Hindi commercial film is people who are in the middle or lower-middle-income groups. But more important than them are the people who live below the poverty line. It's very strange, but most of the people who do odd jobs, or even beggars, will keep their money to see the first show of the new releases. In fact I played a character like that. She was a rag-picker, and whatever money she got from selling rags she would stuff in her blouse, so that she didn't have to give it to her father or mother. She would then use that money to see the first show of the first week of an Amitabh Bachan film. It really happens; it's not a far-fetched imaginary fantasy or some funny incident. It's the truth.

Smita Patil did believe that audiences went to films to enjoy their own fantasies.

> You get to see everything in a three-hour film. You get to see fantastic songs and dances and pretty-looking heroines wearing clothes that these people would

never dream of wearing. So it's a fantasy-based cinema. You have fights and violence, you have sex, and you have everything. You go in, and for three hours you are lost, away from the drudgery of every-day life. And that's it, there is no other form of entertainment.

Besides entertaining, Indian films do provide a common link between different regions and communities and promote a national language. The colloquial Hindustani of the Bombay movies is accepted by cinema-goers throughout India, whereas the stilted, classical Hindi the government has spent millions of rupees ramming down the nation's throat is resented in many areas. Television is now spreading rapidly in India, and Rajiv Gandhi hopes that if it remains under government control, it, too, will become a unifying force. The programmes have a strong middle-class bias and are peppered with advertisements for products which are often beyond the reach of poorer Indians. Inder Gujral, a former Minister of Information and Broadcasting, fears that such programmes could be dangerously divisive.

Because a television set is expensive, almost every family which invests in one spends a great deal of time around it. Since the soap-operas have come, since the serials have come, and the advertisements too, consumerism which is much more dangerous than consumerism elsewhere is growing. We ourselves confess that our poverty, our unemployment, our youth problems are serious. Now we expose this section of society every evening to the glamour of good shampoos and good lipsticks and so on. That's something which creates havoc. I keep watching my mother's young maid. By the time the television comes on, she is so restless to see it. Then I watch this young child from time to time changing her hairstyle, sometimes taking my wife's lipsticks. I don't blame her; in fact, I sympathise with her. This young girl sees that this is a totally different type of life from the life she has been used to, and she thinks that she has suddenly been injected into a heaven which doesn't exist around her.

Television and radio are both run by the government, and that limits the role they can play in preserving a healthy democracy. The Indian press, on the other hand, must be among the most free and lively in the Third World. It does act as a watchdog on the government, which is essential if democracy is to survive in India. There has been an explosion of papers and magazines in both English and Indian languages over the last fifteen years, and journalism has become much more rigorous. But Arun Shourie, one of the pioneers of investigative journalism in India, is surprisingly critical of the Indian press.

> What people regard as the good things the press does are the work of very few people in very small parts of the press. The others don't take their stories up and don't follow them up as they might in other countries. There is another problem. The type of things which are being written about even good individuals are shocking. We do have a good defamation law, but you can't get a conviction in court for ten or fifteen years, so the press does get away with things. Yes, there is no majority in the press that the rulers have by which they can cow down all sections of the press, in the same way that they can cow down Parliament. Yes, appointments in the press are not made by the ruling party, as are for instance appointments of judges. But I would not say the press was in a much healthier position than other institutions.

So many Indians, like Arun Shourie, compare their country and its institutions with other more orderly countries. But India is one country which can live with a certain amount of chaos. It might be described as a functioning anarchy. Professor Rajni Kothari points out that India has never been a well-defined, centralised nation.

> This is the only major culture and civilisation in the world which really didn't have a centre. The contrast with China is most clear. The Chinese identified them-selves with a clear centre, an empire and an emperor, and there was nothing like that in India. So to that extent, the coming of the British and then the national

movement can be considered to be the first steps in the direction of bringing together the tremendous plurality and diversity of the country into a common framework. But Indian nationalism has always flourished through the acceptance of a plural society. That, in fact, is why the interest in nationalism and democracy run side by side. I have constantly maintained that this country was always inherently fertile ground for liberal institutions. It is not as if the British brought them to us.

A plural society can never be a neat affair; but it can be very strong. The Afghans, the Moghuls and the British all tried to put their stamp on India; but they found that it was like punching cotton wool. They made an impact, but they could not dent the essential India whose culture has the inner strength to resist invasions, even to be generous to them.

At the height of the British Raj, Rabindranath Tagore wrote: 'Today the West has opened its doors and thence come gifts. Giving and taking, all will be welcome on the shores of India, where men of all races come together.' India is still taking 'gifts' from the West. But are we prepared to take the wisdom that India's ancient and unique civilisation can give us? Do we welcome all to our shores?

FURTHER READING

AKBAR, M. J. *India: the siege within* Penguin Books, 1985.

BRECHER, M. *Nehru: a political biography* Oxford U.P., 1959.

Cambridge history of India: Vol VI: the Indian empire edited by H. H. Dodwell New Delhi: S. Chand, rev. edn., 1987

GOPAL, S. *Jawaharlal Nehru: a biography: Vol II: 1947–1956* Cape, 1979.

HIRO, D. *Inside India today* Routledge, rev. edn., 1978.

KUMAR, R. *Essays in the social history of modern India* Oxford U.P., 1983.

MASANI, Z. *Indira Gandhi: a biography* Hamilton, 1975.

MAXWELL, N. *India's China war* Penguin, 1972,.

MEHTA, V. *A family affair: India under three prime ministers* Oxford U.P., 1982

TULLY M. AND JACOB, S. *Amritsar: Mrs Gandhi's last battle* Cape, 1985.

ZIEGLER, P. *Mountbatten: the official biography* Collins, 1985.

INDEX